Mometrix
TEST PREPARATION

Florida
Grade 3 Mathematics Test Prep Workbook Answer Key

DEAR FUTURE EXAM SUCCESS STORY

First of all, **THANK YOU** for purchasing Mometrix study materials!

Second, congratulations! You are one of the few determined test-takers who are committed to doing whatever it takes to excel on your exam. **You have come to the right place.** We developed these study materials with one goal in mind: to deliver you the information you need in a format that's concise and easy to use.

In addition to optimizing your guide for the content of the test, we've outlined our recommended steps for breaking down the preparation process into small, attainable goals so you can make sure you stay on track.

We've also analyzed the entire test-taking process, identifying the most common pitfalls and showing how you can overcome them and be ready for any curveball the test throws you.

Standardized testing is one of the biggest obstacles on your road to success, which only increases the importance of doing well in the high-pressure, high-stakes environment of test day. Your results on this test could have a significant impact on your future, and this guide provides the information and practical advice to help you achieve your full potential on test day.

Your success is our success

We would love to hear from you! If you would like to share the story of your exam success or if you have any questions or comments in regard to our products, please contact us at **800-673-8175** or **support@mometrix.com**.

Thanks again for your business and we wish you continued success!

Sincerely,
The Mometrix Test Preparation Team

Written and edited by the Mometrix Exam Secrets Test Prep Team
Printed in the United States of America

TABLE OF CONTENTS

Workbook Answers

Chapter 1—Place Value and Number Sense

Lesson 1

Finding Shape Patterns

1.

2.

3.

4.

5.

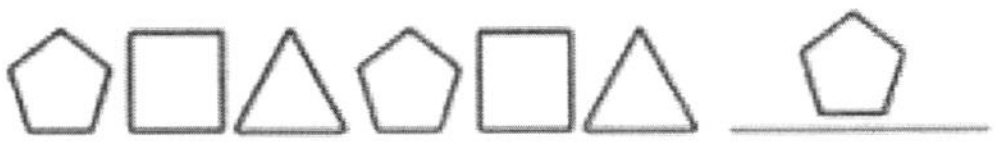

6.

7.

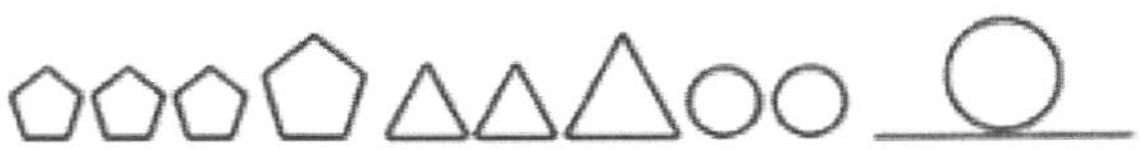

8.

Lesson 2

Even and Odd Single-Digit and Two-Digit Numbers

1. even
2. odd
3. even
4. even
5. odd
6. even
7. odd
8. odd
9. even
10. odd
11. odd
12. even
13. odd
14. even
15. even
16. even
17. odd
18. odd
19. even
20. even
21. odd
22. odd
23. even
24. even

Even and Odd Three-Digit Numbers

1. odd
2. even
3. even
4. odd
5. odd
6. even
7. odd
8. even
9. even
10. even
11. odd
12. odd
13. even
14. odd
15. odd
16. even
17. even
18. even
19. even
20. even
21. odd
22. odd
23. odd
24. even

Lesson 3

Rounding to the Nearest 100

1. 300
2. 900
3. 300
4. 100
5. 200
6. 800
7. 800
8. 100
9. 800
10. 400
11. 300
12. 300
13. 600
14. 1,000
15. 200
16. 300
17. 400
18. 700
19. 700
20. 500
21. 200
22. 800
23. 300
24. 200
25. 800
26. 200
27. 800
28. 300

Lesson 4

Rounding to the Nearest 1,000

1. 8,000
2. 1,000
3. 2,000
4. 9,000
5. 1,000
6. 6,000
7. 4,000
8. 9,000
9. 2,000
10. 7,000
11. 2,000
12. 5,000
13. 7,000
14. 4,000
15. 7,000
16. 9,000
17. 1,000
18. 5,000
19. 5,000
20. 2,000
21. 2,000
22. 1,000
23. 2,000
24. 5,000
25. 1,000
26. 9,000
27. 8,000
28. 3,000

Lesson 5

Finding Number Patterns 1

1.	10	20	30	**(78)**	50	60
2.	5	10	**(34)**	20	25	30
3.	2	4	**(15)**	8	10	12
4.	8	**(2)**	24	32	40	48
5.	3	5	7	**(8)**	9	11
6.	50	60	**(9)**	80	90	100
7.	55	65	75	85	95	**(3)**
8.	**(5)**	8	10	12	14	16
9.	3	5	7	9	11	**(89)**

Finding Number Patterns 2

1. 22
2. 6
3. 16
4. 60
5. 20
6. 96
7. 42
8. 7
9. 540
10. 145

Lesson 6

Place Value by 10s

1. 24
2. 43
3. 39
4. 66
5. 59
6. 86

Lesson 7

Place Value by 100s

1. 129
2. 235
3. 254
4. 325
5. 507

Lesson 8

Place Value by 1,000s

1. 1,347
2. 3,232
3. 2,459
4. 4,157
5. 3,175

Lesson 9

Least to Greatest

1.	4,818	4,982	14,818
2.	880	1,251	1,900
3.	1,210	1,541	1,780
4.	50	74	129
5.	815	1,520	3,500
6.	3,400	5,800	9,570
7.	10	100	1,000
8.	5	330	4,500
9.	250	275	300
10.	16	25	54

Lesson 10
Comparing Numbers

No.	Answer	No.	Answer
1.	>	11.	>
2.	>	12.	<
3.	<	13.	>
4.	<	14.	=
5.	<	15.	>
6.	=	16.	>
7.	=	17.	<
8.	<	18.	=
9.	>	19.	<
10.	<	20.	<

Lesson 11
Converting Symbols to Numbers

1. 1,221
2. 2,142
3. 333
4. 3,321
5. 2,340

Lesson 12

Place Value up to 100,000

1.	3 Hundred Thousands	9 Ten Thousands	2 Thousands	5 Hundreds	9 Tens	9 Ones
2.	4 Hundred Thousands	1 Ten Thousands	5 Thousands	6 Hundreds	7 Tens	5 Ones
3.	7 Hundred Thousands	2 Ten Thousands	6 Thousands	2 Hundreds	1 Tens	1 Ones
4.	1 Hundred Thousands	8 Ten Thousands	6 Thousands	4 Hundreds	5 Tens	2 Ones

Lesson 13

Composing Numbers Using Expanded Form

1. 1,263

2. 9,432

3. 7,086

4. 540

5. 3,323

Chapter 2—Addition

Lesson 1

2-Digit Addition – Regrouping 1

1. 80	2. 92	3. 70	4. 83
5. 101	6. 114	7. 83	8. 44
9. 71	10. 86	11. 34	12. 53

2-Digit Addition – Regrouping 2

1. 121	2. 52	3. 92	4. 84
5. 113	6. 100	7. 42	8. 122
9. 93	10. 30	11. 91	12. 53
13. 91	14. 92	15. 131	16. 122
17. 91	18. 82	19. 133	

2-Digit Addition – Regrouping 3

1. 172	2. 134	3. 144	4. 131
5. 60	6. 165	7. 51	8. 151
9. 113	10. 92	11. 120	12. 132
13. 84	14. 105	15. 31	16. 97
17. 60	18. 60	19. 84	

Lesson 2

Symbol Addition 1

1. 100 + 10 + 10 + 1 = 121

2. 100 + 1 + 1 + 1 + 1 + 1 = 105

3. 100 + 100 + 100 + 100 + 100 + 10 = 510

4. 10 + 10 + 10 + 10 + 1 + 1 = 42

5. 100 + 100 + 10 + 10 + 10 + 10 = 240

6. 100 + 10 + 1 + 1 + 1 +1 = 114

7. 100 + 100 + 100 + 10 + 1 + 1 = 312

8. 100 + 10 + 10 + 10 +10 + 1 = 141

Symbol Addition 2

1. 1,000 + 100 + 10 + 1 + 1 = 1,112

2. 1,000 + 1,000 + 1,000 + 100 + 1 = 3,101

3. 1,000 + 100 + 100 + 10 + 1 + 1 = 1,212

4. 1,000 + 1,000 + 1,000 + 1,000 + 100 = 4,100

5. 1,000 + 1,000 + 100 + 100 + 10 + 10 = 2,220

6. 100 + 10 + 10 + 1 + 1 + 1 = 123

7. 1,000 + 1,000 + 100 + 10 + 10 + 1 = 2,121

8. 100 + 100 + 100 + 10 + 10 + 1 = 321

Lesson 3

Adding 3-Digit Numbers 1

1. 1,806	2. 892	3. 1,330	4. 923
5. 1,322	6. 831	7. 389	8. 1,054
9. 1,580	10. 204	11. 964	12. 876
13. 1,364	14. 648	15. 714	16. 1,030
17. 1,046	18. 562	19. 975	

Adding 3-Digit Numbers 2

1. 1,773	2. 2,782	3. 851	4. 1,437
5. 1,648	6. 1,286	7. 899	8. 1,208
9. 2,228	10. 1,511	11. 1,054	12. 1,947
13. 1,673	14. 1,395	15. 722	

Adding 3-Digit Numbers 3

1. 2,387	2. 1,190	3. 3,055	4. 2,254
5. 1,569	6. 2,266	7. 1,619	8. 2,094
9. 1,536	10. 2,321	11. 1,485	12. 1,481

Lesson 4

Fill in the Blanks

Fill in the blanks to complete each problem.

1. **1** 2 4 + 1 9 **1** 3 1 5	2. 2 **3** 9 + **6** 3 2 8 7 1	3. 3 4 8 + **6** 3 **1** 9 7 9	4. 6 **2** 3 + 2 **2** 2 8 4 5
5. **1** 3 7 + 4 **4** 7 5 8 4	6. 5 8 **3** + **3** 9 1 9 7 4	7. 3 7 5 + 1 **7** **5** 5 8 0	8. **1** 1 5 + 1 2 **2** 2 3 7
9. **4** 2 4 + 1 2 3 5 4 7	10. 5 **2** 4 + **2** 6 1 7 8 5	11. **2** 3 4 + 1 6 **2** 3 9 6	

Lesson 5

Adding 4-Digit Numbers 1

1. 5,501	2. 7,061	3. 8,636	4. 8,023
5. 8,711	6. 9,482	7. 4,121	8. 15,195
9. 18,911	10. 6,526	11. 14,723	12. 8,041
13. 7,905	14. 10,164	15. 4,399	

Adding 4-Digit Numbers 2

1. 7,641	2. 10,626	3. 11,044	4. 21,672
5. 19,295	6. 22,701	7. 19,214	8. 23,256
9. 18,628	10. 11,171	11. 9,686	12. 21,667

Lesson 6

Addition Squares 1

1.

1	5	**6**
5	2	**7**
6	**7**	**13**

2.

2	8	**10**
8	9	**17**
10	**17**	**27**

3.

6	3	**9**
3	6	**9**
9	**9**	**18**

4.

2	15	**17**
15	2	**17**
17	**17**	**34**

5.

25	4	**29**
4	10	**14**
29	**14**	**43**

6.

1	8	**9**
8	40	**48**
9	**48**	**57**

ADDITION SQUARES 2

1.

10	3	**13**
3	10	**13**
13	**13**	**<u>26</u>**

2.

5	8	**13**
8	5	**13**
13	**13**	**<u>26</u>**

3.

1	7	**8**
7	1	**8**
8	**8**	**<u>16</u>**

4.

3	6	**9**
6	12	**18**
9	**18**	**<u>27</u>**

5.

70	13	**83**
13	45	**58**
83	**58**	**<u>141</u>**

6.

2	36	**38**
36	2	**38**
38	**38**	**<u>76</u>**

Chapter 3—Subtraction

Lesson 1

Subtracting 2-Digit Numbers 1

1. 13	2. 5	3. 5	4. 36
5. 37	6. 20	7. 22	8. 22
9. 27	10. 14	11. 59	12. 43

Subtracting 2-Digit Numbers 2

1. 2	2. 7	3. 7	4. 4
5. 53	6. 61	7. 6	8. 48
9. 68	10. 40	11. 8	12. 60
13. 35	14. 48	15. 17	16. 8
17. 36	18. 31	19. 14	

Subtracting 2-Digit Numbers 3

1. 44	2. 45	3. 23	4. 8
5. 23	6. 55	7. 9	8. 8
9. 52	10. 41	11. 33	12. 36
13. 28	14. 61	15. 35	16. 55
17. 2	18. 18	19. 30	

Lesson 2

Subtracting 3-Digit Numbers 1

1. 28	2. 37	3. 66	4. 42
5. 526	6. 612	7. 523	8. 472
9. 678	10. 378	11. 65	12. 605
13. 341	14. 483	15. 157	16. 77
17. 361	18. 313	19. 87	

Subtracting 3-Digit Numbers 2

1. 380	2. 658	3. 204	4. 261
5. 457	6. 3	7. 204	8. 227
9. 339	10. 769	11. 359	12. 338
13. 551	14. 249	15. 769	16. 555
17. 520	18. 166	19. 794	

Subtracting 3-Digit Numbers 3

1. 182	2. 119	3. 299	4. 106
5. 87	6. 156	7. 155	8. 260
9. 77	10. 110	11. 425	12. 55
13. 208	14. 234	15. 23	16. 236
17. 502	18. 592	19. 104	

Lesson 3

Subtraction Sentences 1

1. 85	2. 32	3. 136	4. 42
5. 81	6. 53	7. 83	8. 73
9. 112	10. 74	11. 20	12. 61
13. 37	14. 160	15. 40	16. 57
17. 92	18. 16	19. 356	20. 30

Subtraction Sentences 2

1. 105	2. 80	3. 170	4. 30
5. 135	6. 20	7. 119	8. 199
9. 41	10. 86	11. 50	12. 40
13. 60	14. 15	15. 30	16. 30
17. 187	18. 75	19. 180	20. 161

Lesson 4

Regroup Over Two Zeros

1. 194	2. 591	3. 122	4. 793
5. 377	6. 881	7. 587	8. 314
9. 233	10. 195	11. 619	12. 214
13. 55	14. 66	15. 378	16. 46
17. 473	18. 95	19. 66	

Lesson 5

Subtracting 4-Digit Numbers 1

1. 2,071	2. 2,009	3. 8,920	4. 2,980
5. 3,331	6. 4,091	7. 5,071	8. 4,334
9. 2,781	10. 5,565	11. 7,573	12. 1,121
13. 1,213	14. 1,151		

Subtracting 4-Digit Numbers 2

1. 3,366	2. 904	3. 2,459	4. 154
5. 861	6. 1,248	7. 3,761	8. 3,626
9. 5,071	10. 1,925	11. 2,075	12. 111
13. 3,454	14. 320		

Subtracting 4-Digit Numbers 3

1. 1,889	2. 573	3. 1,044	4. 2,589
5. 3,679	6. 19	7. 889	8. 489
9. 1,175	10. 2,689	11. 1,230	12. 6,495
13. 3,353	14. 3,984		

Subtracting 4-Digit Numbers 4

1. 4,690	2. 5,844	3. 2,045	4. 2,571
5. 1,784	6. 4,222	7. 5,406	8. 5,897
9. 6,122	10. 5,009	11. 5,329	12. 408
13. 9,036	14. 676		

Chapter 4—Multiplication

Lesson 1

Multiplication Rules

1. $3 \times 2 = 6$

2 + 2 + 2 + 2 = 6

2. $3 \times 4 = 12$

4 + 4 + 4 = 12

3. $4 \times 4 = 16$

4 + 4 + 4 + 4 = 16

4. $4 \times 5 = 20$

5 + 5 + 5 + 5 = 20

5. $3 \times 8 = 24$

8 + 8 + 8 = 24

6. $4 \times 10 = 40$

10 + 10 + 10 + 10 = 40

7. $2 \times 6 = 12$

6 + 6 = 12

8. $3 \times 6 = 18$

6 + 6 + 6 = 18

Lesson 2

Multiplication by 1

1. 0	2. 4	3. 1	4. 9	5. 9	6. 6	7. 2
8. 8	9. 6	10. 0	11. 3	12. 4	13. 6	14. 5
15. 3	16. 0	17. 2	18. 7	19. 8	20. 7	21. 0

Lesson 3

Multiplication by 2

1. 18	2. 8	3. 16	4. 14	5. 18	6. 10	7. 2
8. 4	9. 6	10. 6	11. 18	12. 16	13. 14	14. 10
15. 0	16. 12	17. 16	18. 10	19. 8	20. 2	21. 12

LESSON 4
MULTIPLICATION BY 3

1. 6	2. 27	3. 6	4. 21	5. 24	6. 12	7. 27
8. 24	9. 21	10. 24	11. 18	12. 12	13. 15	14. 9
15. 3	16. 3	17. 0	18. 15	19. 27	20. 15	21. 18

LESSON 5
MULTIPLICATION BY 4

1. 4	2. 0	3. 20	4. 12	5. 4	6. 32	7. 12
8. 28	9. 8	10. 8	11. 36	12. 20	13. 32	14. 4
15. 0	16. 24	17. 36	18. 28	19. 12	20. 24	21. 36

LESSON 6
MULTIPLICATION BY 5

1. 15	2. 10	3. 35	4. 30	5. 0	6. 5	7. 30
8. 40	9. 35	10. 40	11. 30	12. 25	13. 5	14. 45
15. 10	16. 40	17. 45	18. 15	19. 45	20. 10	21. 0

LESSON 7
MULTIPLICATION BY 6

1. 0	2. 54	3. 18	4. 36	5. 12	6. 6	7. 42
8. 18	9. 36	10. 6	11. 30	12. 24	13. 0	14. 30
15. 54	16. 12	17. 30	18. 18	19. 48	20. 42	21. 0

Lesson 8

Multiplication by 7

1. 14	2. 0	3. 35	4. 7	5. 42	6. 14	7. 21
8. 21	9. 63	10. 56	11. 28	12. 42	13. 28	14. 35
15. 14	16. 42	17. 7	18. 49	19. 56	20. 7	21. 42

Lesson 9

Multiplication by 8

1. 56	2. 32	3. 8	4. 16	5. 0	6. 40	7. 72
8. 24	9. 24	10. 0	11. 16	12. 40	13. 16	14. 56
15. 40	16. 72	17. 64	18. 32	19. 32	20. 16	21. 24

Lesson 10

Multiplication by 9

1. 9	2. 36	3. 63	4. 81	5. 27	6. 45	7. 9
8. 9	9. 54	10. 18	11. 54	12. 72	13. 63	14. 45
15. 36	16. 36	17. 0	18. 54	19. 81	20. 45	21. 27

Lesson 11

Multiplication Fill in the Blanks

1. 3	2. 4
3. 5	4. 9
5. 5	6. 2
7. 10	8. 8
5. 6	15. 6
9. 6	10. 7

Lesson 12

Multiplication by 10

1. 30	2. 20	3. 50	4. 60
5. 10	6. 50	7. 40	8. 80
9. 70	10. 0	11. 90	12. 20
13. 40	14. 30	15. 90	

Lesson 13

Multiplication by 100

1. 400	2. 200	3. 500	4. 600
5. 100	6. 400	7. 800	8. 900
9. 0	10. 700	11. 300	12. 700
13. 400	14. 300	15. 900	

Lesson 14

2-Digit Multiplication

1. 48	2. 219	3. 120	4. 128
5. 48	6. 63	7. 75	8. 108
9. 49	10. 76		

Chapter 5—Division

Lesson 1

Dividing Objects 1

10 Bananas		**5**
15 Nuts		**3**
9 Cheeses		**3**
14 Bones		**7**
20 Carrots		**5**

DIVIDING OBJECTS 2

÷ 4 = 2

÷ 2 = 4

÷ 5 = 2

÷ 2 = 5

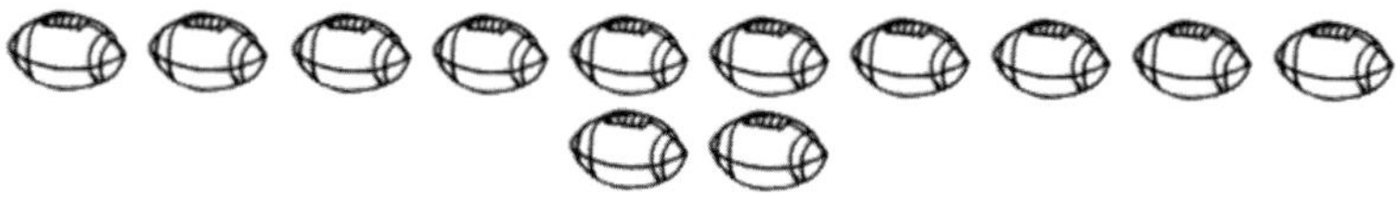

÷ 3 = 4

÷ 2 = 6

÷ 3 = 5

÷ 5 = 3

÷ 5 = 4

÷ 4 = 5

÷ 2 = 10

÷ 8 = 3

÷ 4 = 6

÷ 2 = 12

Lesson 2

Division Wording and Terms

1. 18, 9, 2

2. 16, 4, 4

3. 125, 5, 25

4. 15, 5, 3

5. 100, 10, 10

6. 72, 9, 8

7. 4, 12, 3

8. 5, 30, 6

9. 6, 42, 7

10. 8, 64, 8

11. 2, 10, 5

12. 3, 21, 7

Lesson 3

Dividing by 10 and 100

1. 7
2. 7
3. 46
4. 52
5. 28
6. 37
7. 27
8. 33
9. 22
10. 99
11. 59
12. 82
13. 80
14. 90
15. 30
16. 97
17. 46
18. 95
19. 59
20. 65

Lesson 4

Writing Division

1. $24 \div 8 = 3$, $24 \div 3 = 8$, $24 \div 6 = 4$, $24 \div 4 = 6$

2. $15 \div 3 = 5$, $15 \div 5 = 3$

3. $10 \div 2 = 5$, $10 \div 5 = 2$

4. $50 \div 5 = 10$, $50 \div 10 = 5$

Lesson 5

Basic Division 1

1. 6

2. 5

3. 6

4. 4

5. 4

6. 9

7. 8

8. 9

9. 8

10. 8

Basic Division 2

1. 10

2. 4

3. 5

4. 5

5. 7

6. 1

7. 5

8. 10

9. 3

10. 6

Lesson 6

Divide by 2 Both Ways

1. 20
2. 4
3. 25
4. 15
5. 6
6. 10
7. 5
8. 25
9. 19
10. 12
11. 22
12. 30
13. 10
14. 42
15. 6
16. 18

Lesson 7

Divide by 5 Both Ways

1. 8
2. 18
3. 10
4. 6
5. 3
6. 4
7. 2
8. 10
9. 7
10. 5
11. 17
12. 6
13. 13
14. 18
15. 21
16. 40

Lesson 8

Division Fill in the Blanks 1

1. 14	11. 36
2. 5	12. 6
3. 7	13. 10
4. 10	14. 36
5. 7	15. 5
6. 9	16. 7
7. 18	17. 100
8. 10	18. 10
9. 5	19. 40
10. 4	20. 15

DIVISION FILL IN THE BLANKS 2

1. 30	11. 92
2. 5	12. 9
3. 63	13. 10
4. 29	14. 55
5. 2	15. 6
6. 7	16. 8
7. 48	17. 22
8. 5	18. 7
9. 4	19. 14
10. 3	20. 16

Chapter 6—Fractions

Lesson 1

Identifying Fractions

1. 

2. 

3. 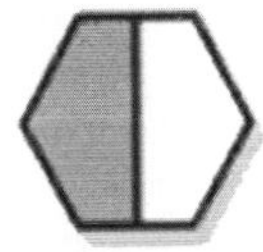

4. 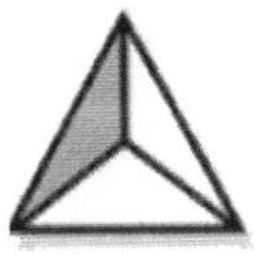

5. 

6. 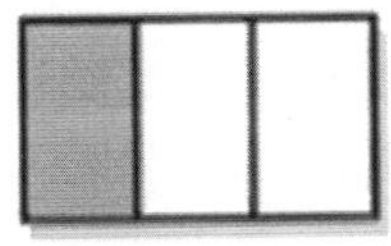

7. 

8. 

9. 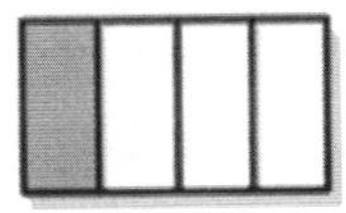

LESSON 2

EXPLAINING FRACTIONS 1

1.	$\frac{1}{4}$	2.	$\frac{2}{6}$
3.	$\frac{2}{8}$	4.	$\frac{4}{15}$
5.	$\frac{6}{8}$	6.	$\frac{7}{10}$
7.	$\frac{5}{12}$	8.	$\frac{9}{15}$

EXPLAINING FRACTIONS 2

1.

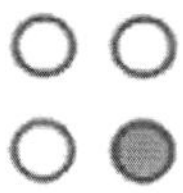

2.

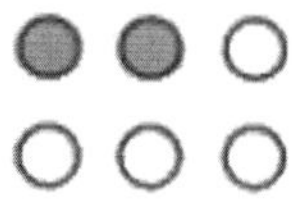

3.

4.

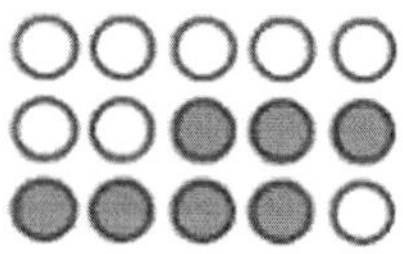

5.

6.

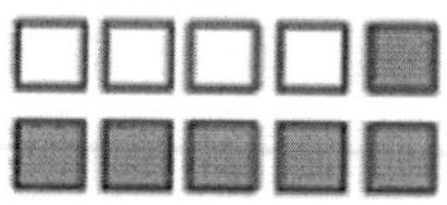

7.

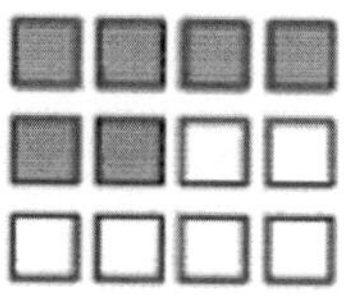

8.

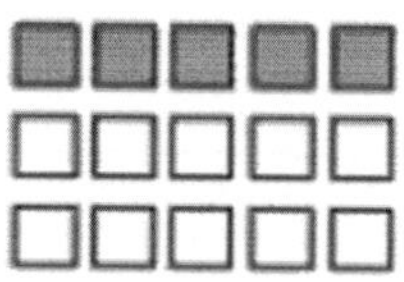

Lesson 3
Matching Fractions 1

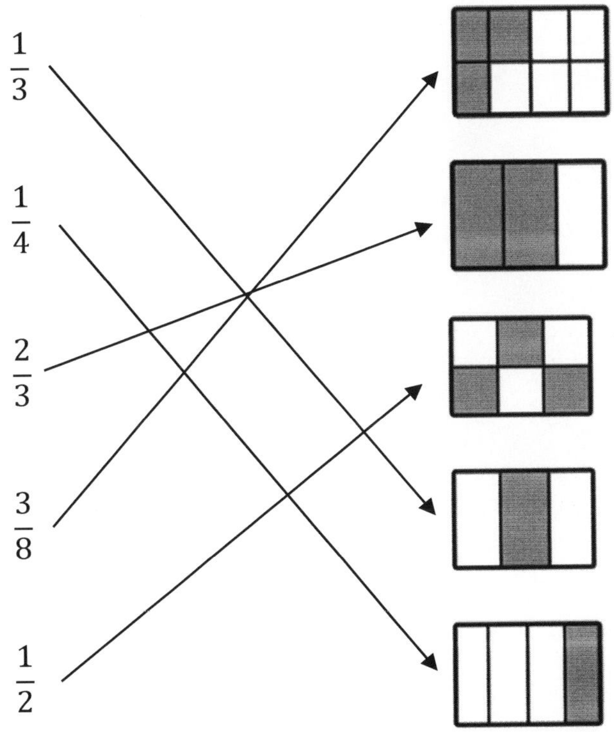

Lesson 4

Writing Fractions 1

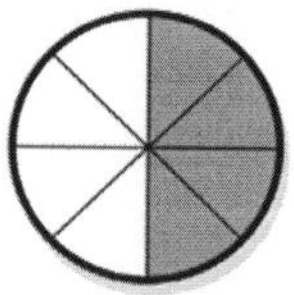 = $\frac{4}{8}$

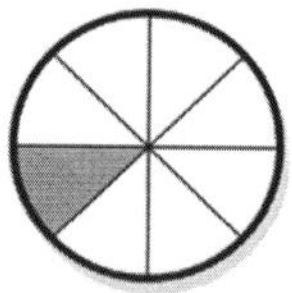 = $\frac{1}{8}$

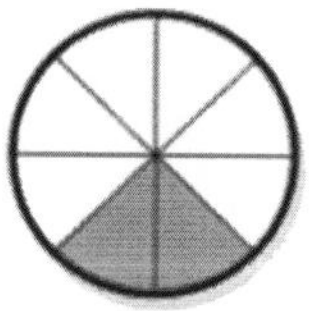 = $\frac{2}{8}$

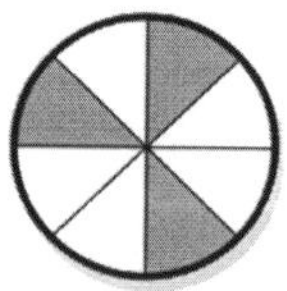 = $\frac{3}{8}$

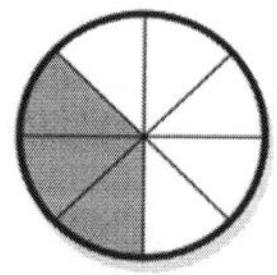 = $\frac{3}{8}$

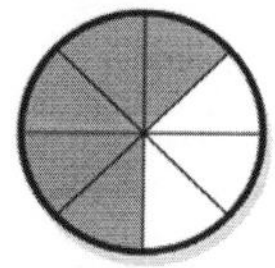 = $\frac{5}{8}$

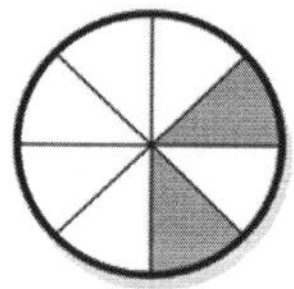 = $\frac{2}{8}$

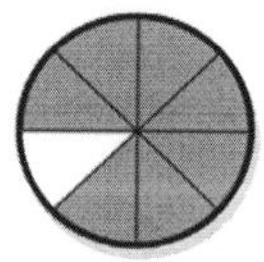 = $\frac{7}{8}$

Writing Fractions 2

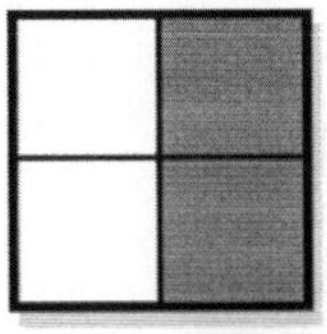 $= \frac{2}{4}$

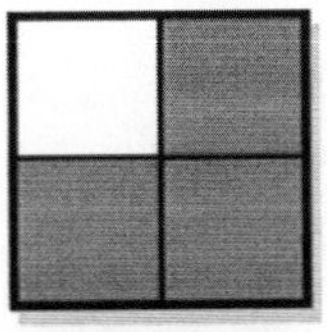 $= \frac{3}{4}$

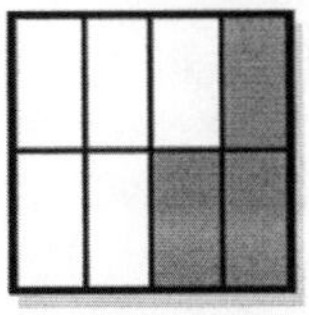 $= \frac{3}{8}$

 $= \frac{7}{8}$

 $= \frac{2}{16}$

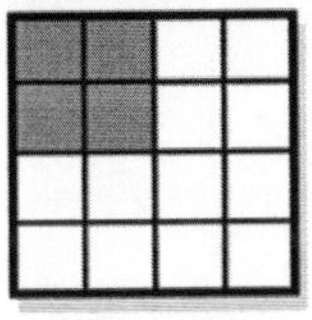 $= \frac{4}{16}$

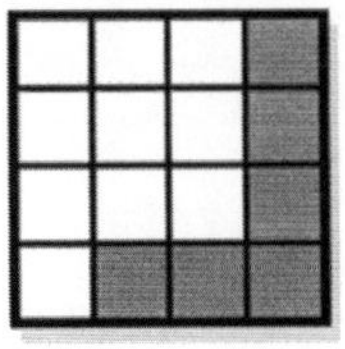 $= \frac{6}{16}$

 $= \frac{9}{16}$

Lesson 5
Making Fractions

$\frac{1}{4}$ = 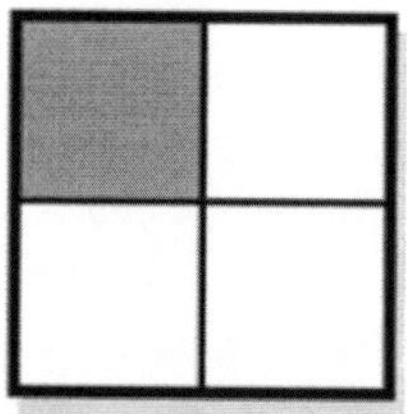

$\frac{1}{2}$ = 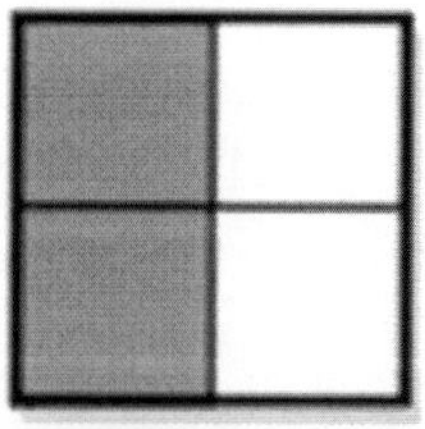

$\frac{3}{8}$ = 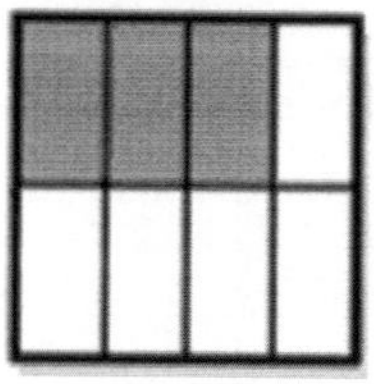

$\frac{5}{8}$ = 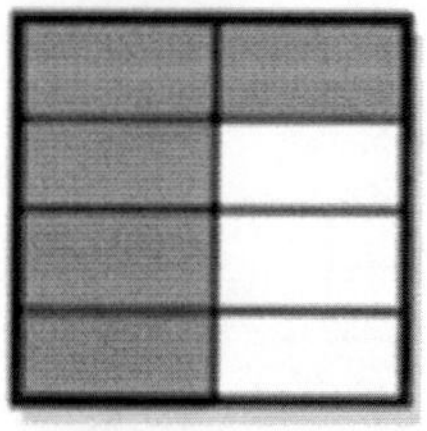

$\frac{5}{16}$ = 

$\frac{9}{16}$ = 

$\frac{2}{16}$ = 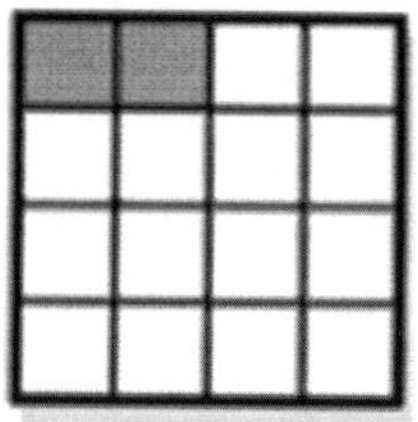

$\frac{7}{16}$ = 

LESSON 6
WHOLE NUMBERS AND FRACTIONS

1.	$1 = \frac{5}{5}$	2.	$1 = \frac{\mathbf{8}}{8}$	3.	$1 = \frac{3}{\mathbf{3}}$
4.	$1 = \frac{\mathbf{14}}{14}$	5.	$1 = \frac{6}{\mathbf{6}}$	6.	$1 = \frac{\mathbf{10}}{10}$

1.	$5 = \frac{5}{1}$	2.	$14 = \frac{\mathbf{14}}{\mathbf{1}}$	3.	$9 = \frac{\mathbf{9}}{\mathbf{1}}$
4.	$72 = \frac{\mathbf{72}}{\mathbf{1}}$	5.	$3 = \frac{\mathbf{3}}{\mathbf{1}}$	6.	$18 = \frac{\mathbf{18}}{\mathbf{1}}$

LESSON 7
IDENTIFYING FRACTIONS

1. $\frac{5}{6}$ 

2. $\frac{1}{3}$ 

3. $\frac{7}{10}$ 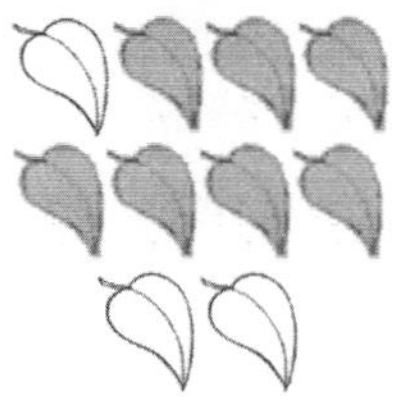

4. $\frac{1}{2}$ 

5. $\frac{1}{3}$ 

6. $\frac{3}{10}$ 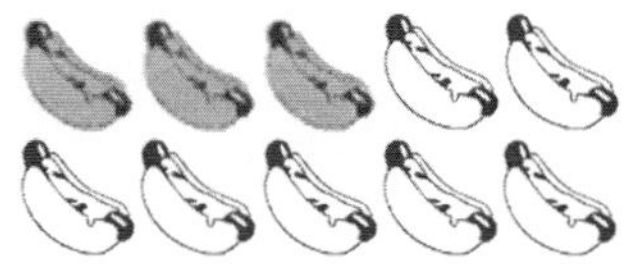

7. $\frac{1}{4}$ 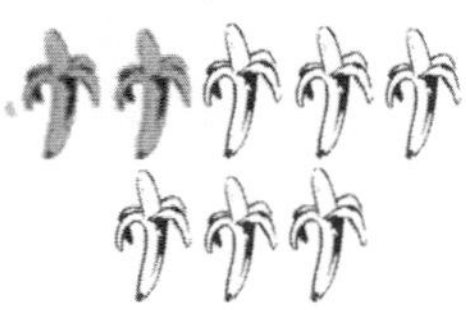

8. $\frac{2}{3}$ 

LESSON 8
COMPARING FRACTIONS

1. 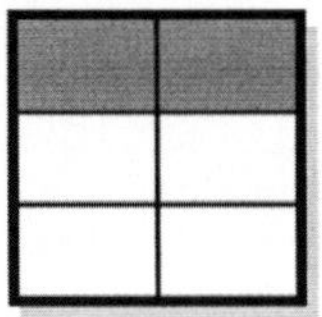 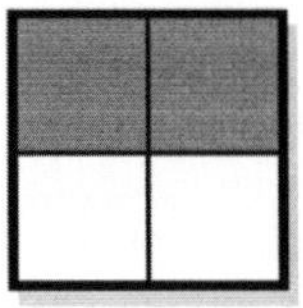

$\frac{2}{6}$ _<_ $\frac{2}{4}$

2. 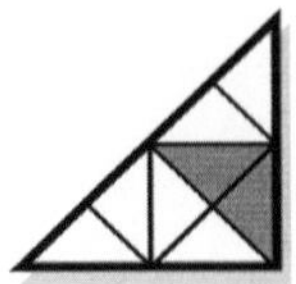 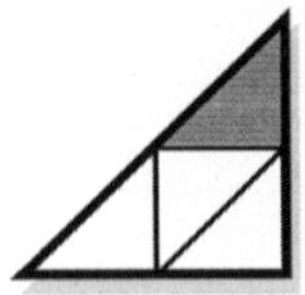

$\frac{2}{8}$ _=_ $\frac{1}{4}$

3. 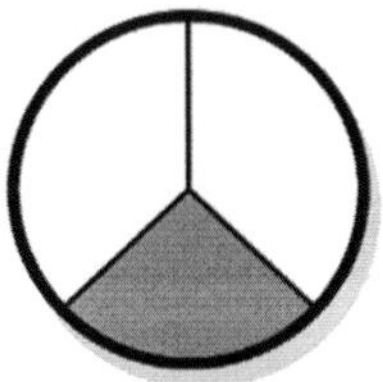 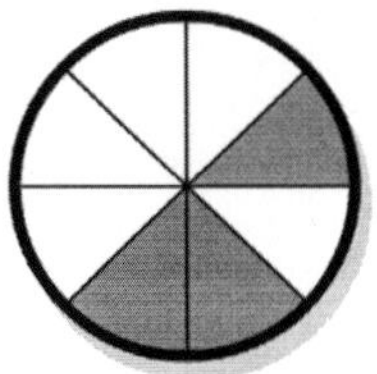

$\frac{1}{3}$ _<_ $\frac{3}{8}$

4. 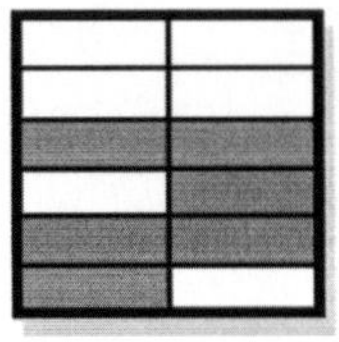 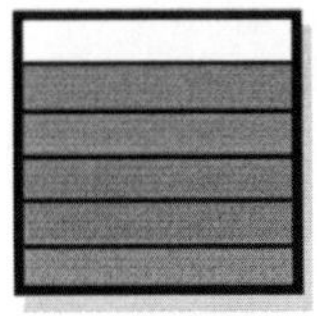

$\frac{6}{12}$ _<_ $\frac{5}{6}$

LESSON 9

CHOOSING FRACTIONS

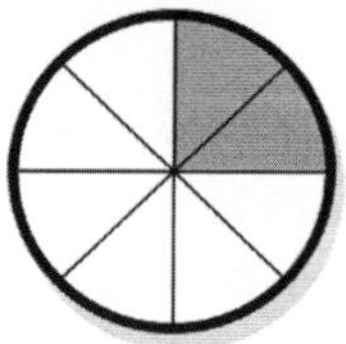 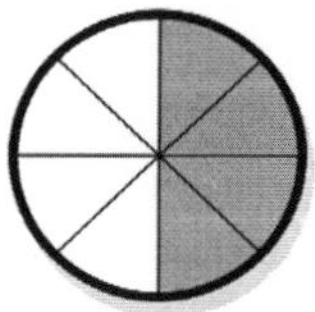

$\frac{2}{8}$ $<$ $\frac{4}{8}$

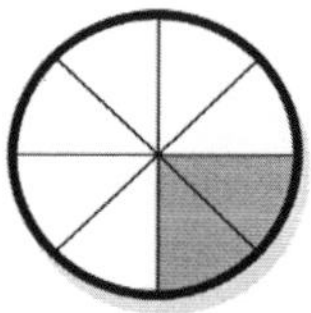 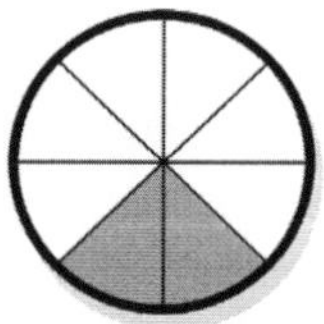

$\frac{2}{8}$ $=$ $\frac{2}{8}$

 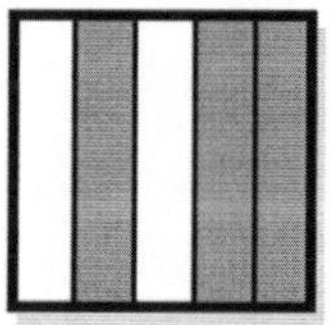

$\frac{2}{5}$ $<$ $\frac{3}{5}$

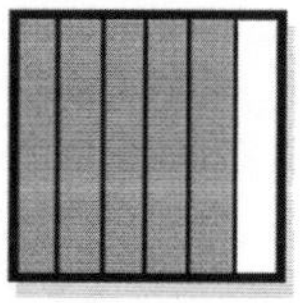 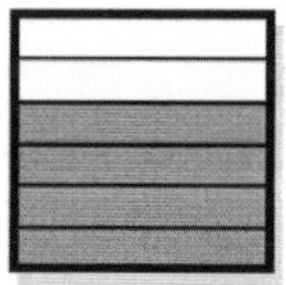

$\frac{5}{6}$ $>$ $\frac{4}{6}$

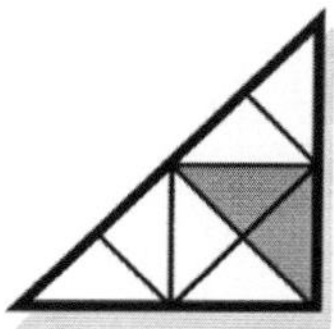 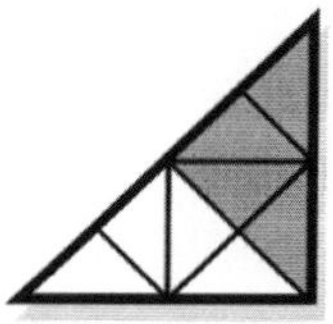

$\frac{1}{4}$ $<$ $\frac{1}{2}$

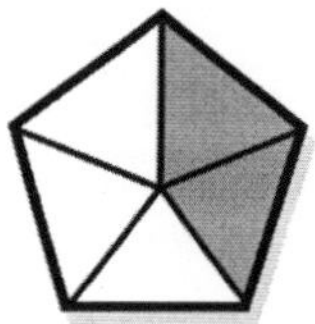 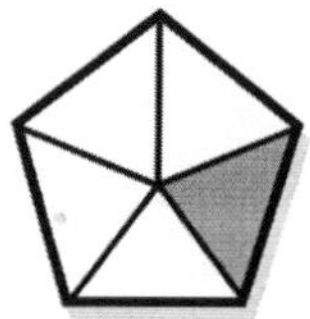

$\frac{2}{5}$ $>$ $\frac{1}{5}$

Lesson 10

Fractions and Values

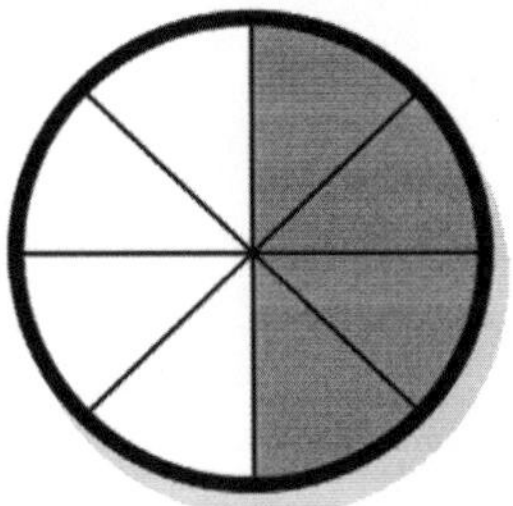

$\frac{3}{4}$ $\frac{1}{2}$ $\frac{1}{8}$

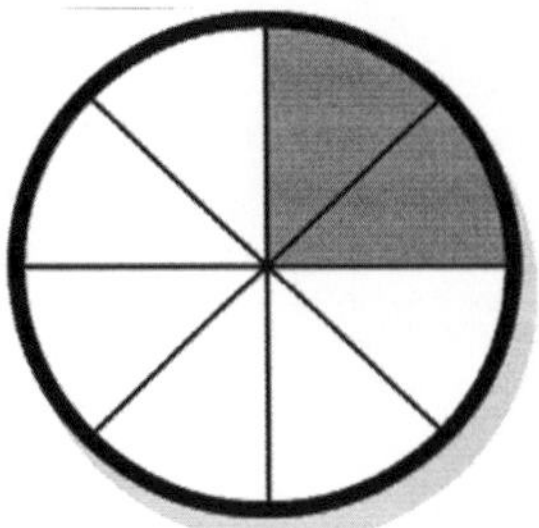

$\frac{1}{2}$ $\frac{1}{8}$ $\frac{1}{4}$

$\frac{3}{8}$ $\frac{1}{2}$ $\frac{2}{4}$

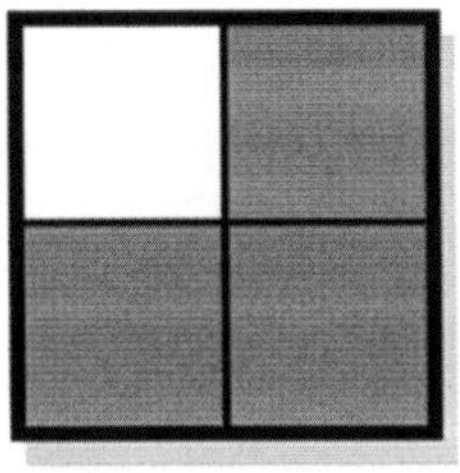

$\frac{3}{4}$ $\frac{1}{2}$ $\frac{1}{8}$

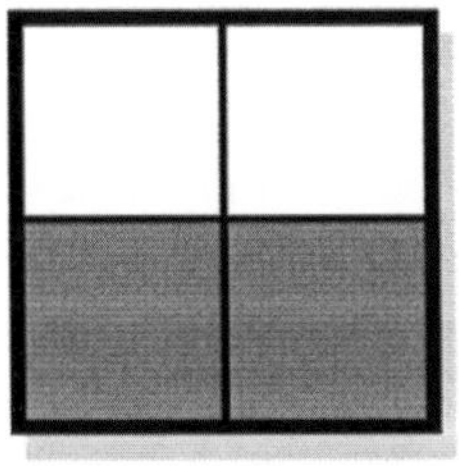

$\frac{1}{2}$ $\frac{3}{4}$ $\frac{1}{4}$

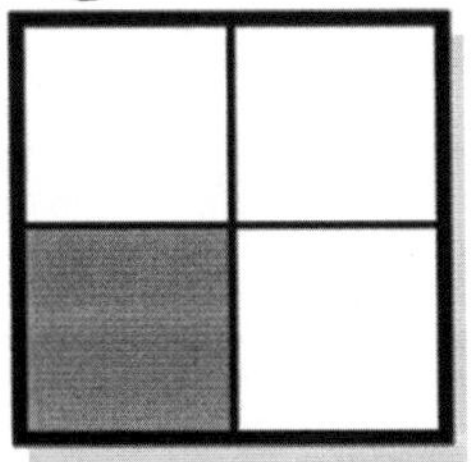

$\frac{2}{3}$ $\frac{1}{2}$ $\frac{1}{4}$

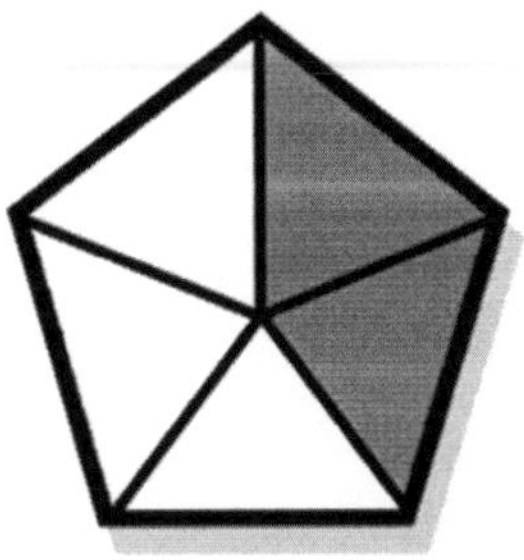

$\frac{3}{4}$ $\frac{2}{5}$ $\frac{1}{8}$

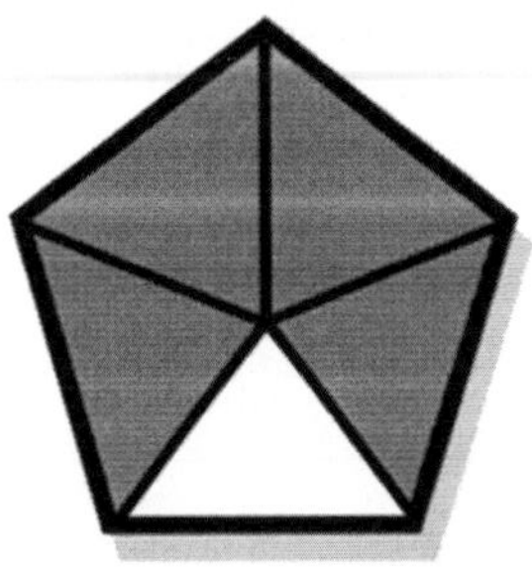

$\frac{4}{5}$ $\frac{1}{4}$ $\frac{3}{5}$

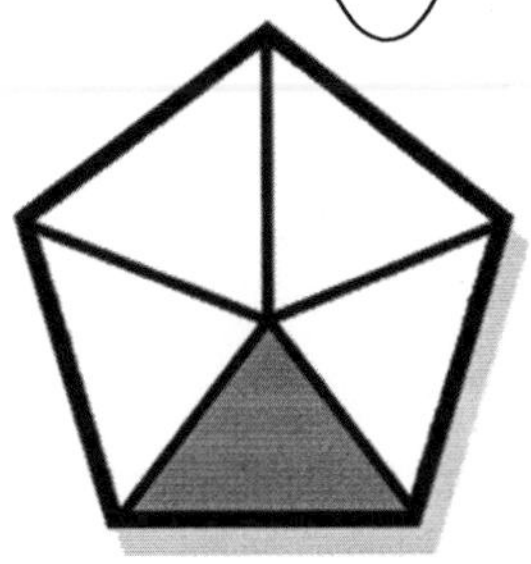

$\frac{3}{5}$ $\frac{1}{3}$ $\frac{1}{5}$

Chapter 7—Graphing

Lesson 1

Creating a Bar Graph 1

Color in a square for each object you see in the picture below.

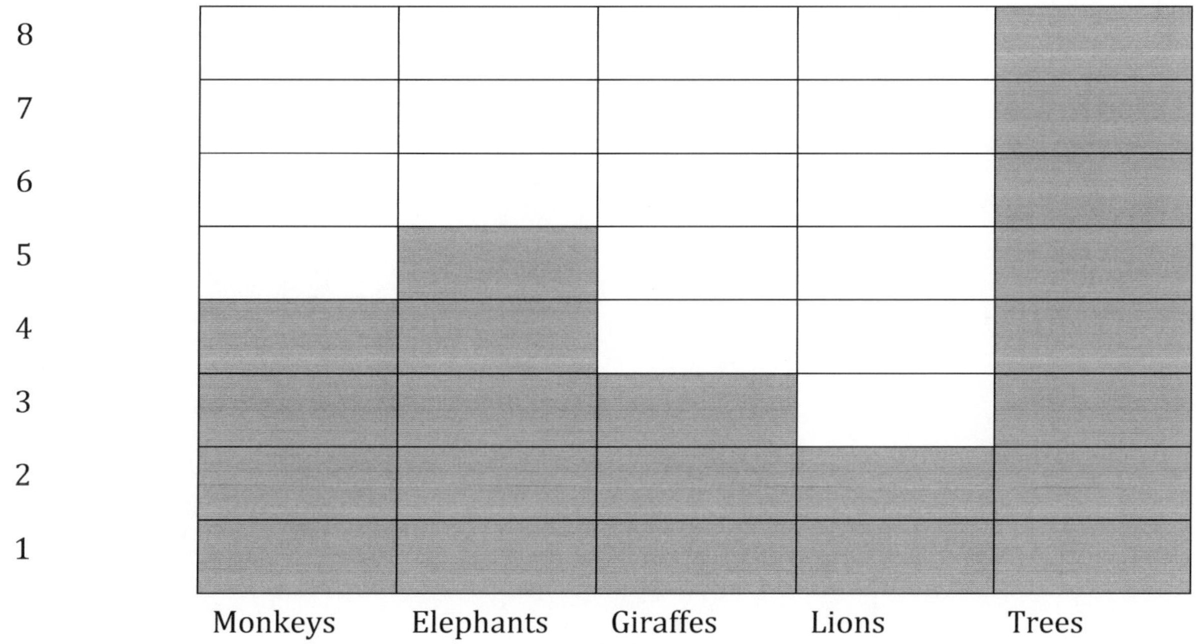

Creating a Bar Graph 1 – Matching Questions

1. 3

2. 5

3. 2

4. 4

5. 5

6. 1

7. 6

Creating a Bar Graph 2

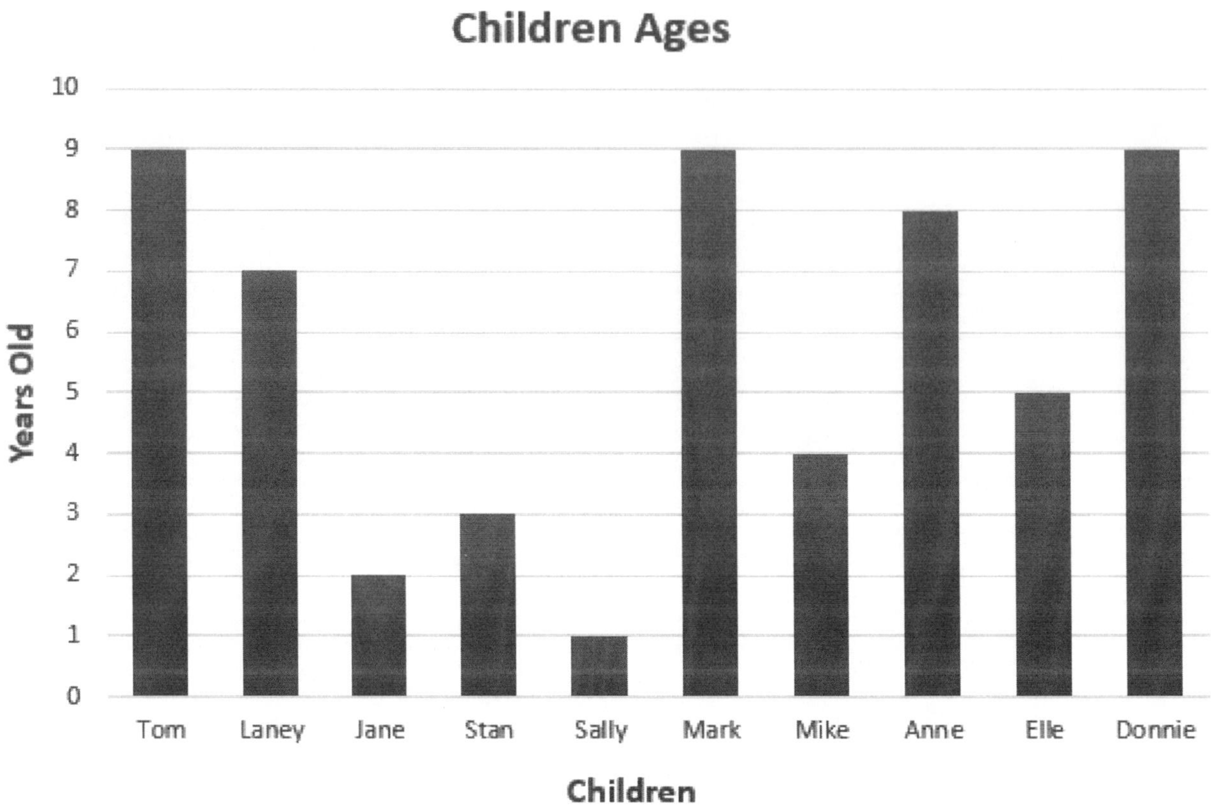

Lesson 2

Reading a Bar Graph

1. Soda

2. Water

3. 2

4. 4

Lesson 3

Word Problems and Tables

1. $50

2. 13 miles

3. 32 pieces of candy

4. 97 cupcakes

Lesson 4
Creating Dot Plots

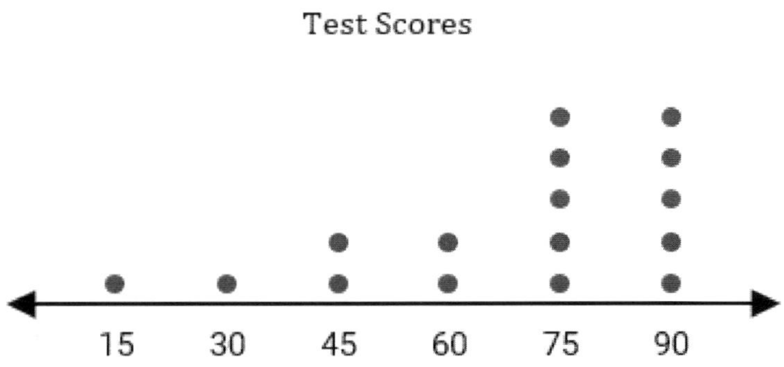

Lesson 5
Reading Dot Plots

1. 12

2. 13, 20

3. 2

4. 7

Lesson 6
Creating Pictographs

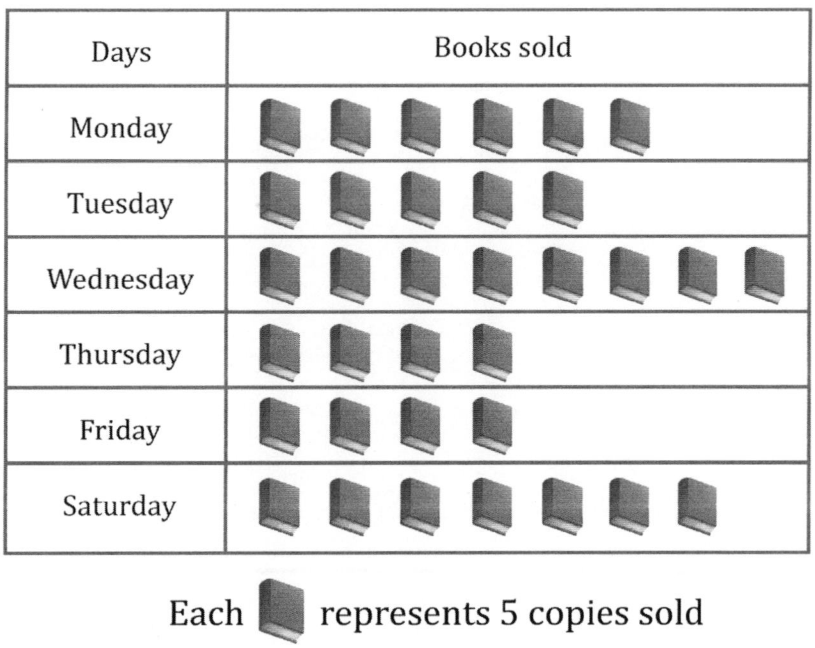

LESSON 7

READING PICTOGRAPHS

1. 120
2. Tuesday and Thursday
3. 520
4. Wednesday

LESSON 8

CREATING A LINE GRAPH

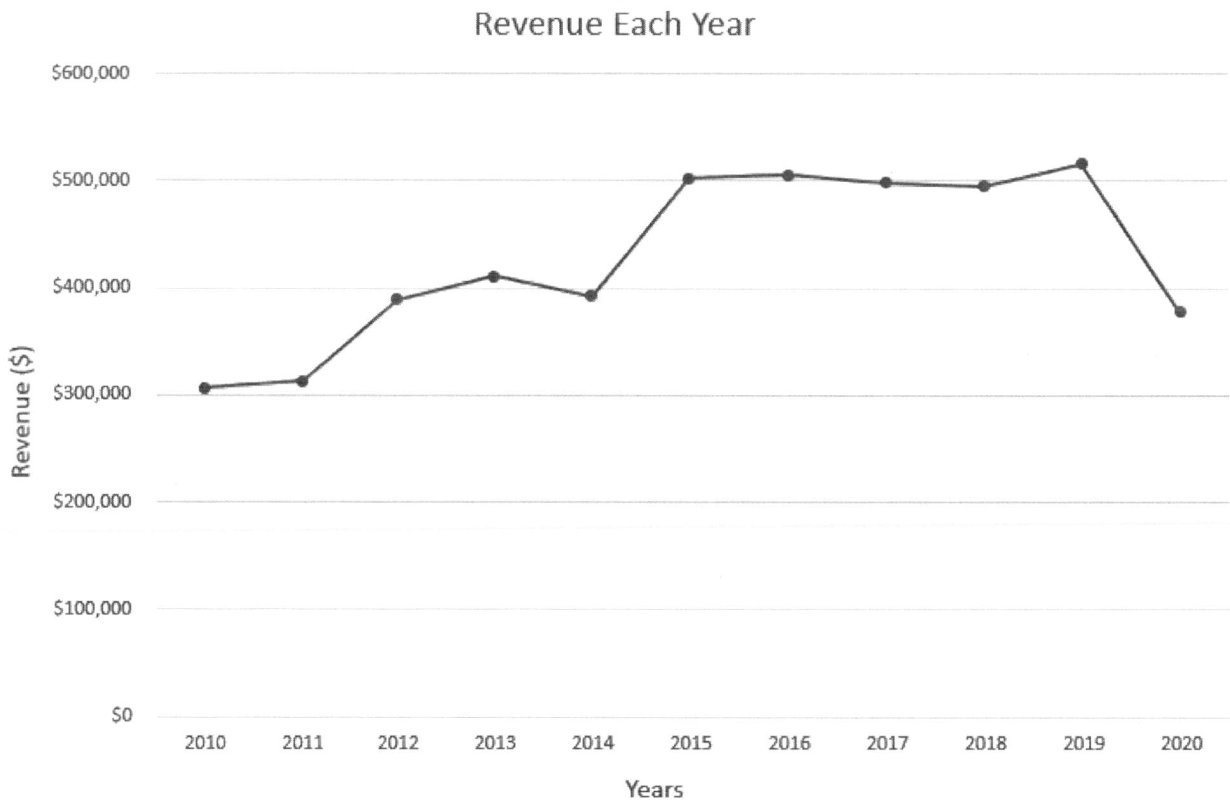

Lesson 9

Reading a Line Graph

1. December
2. July
3. 35 degrees
4. 40-45 degrees
5. 30 degrees
6. Hotter
7. No
8. December

Lesson 10

Creating Pie Charts

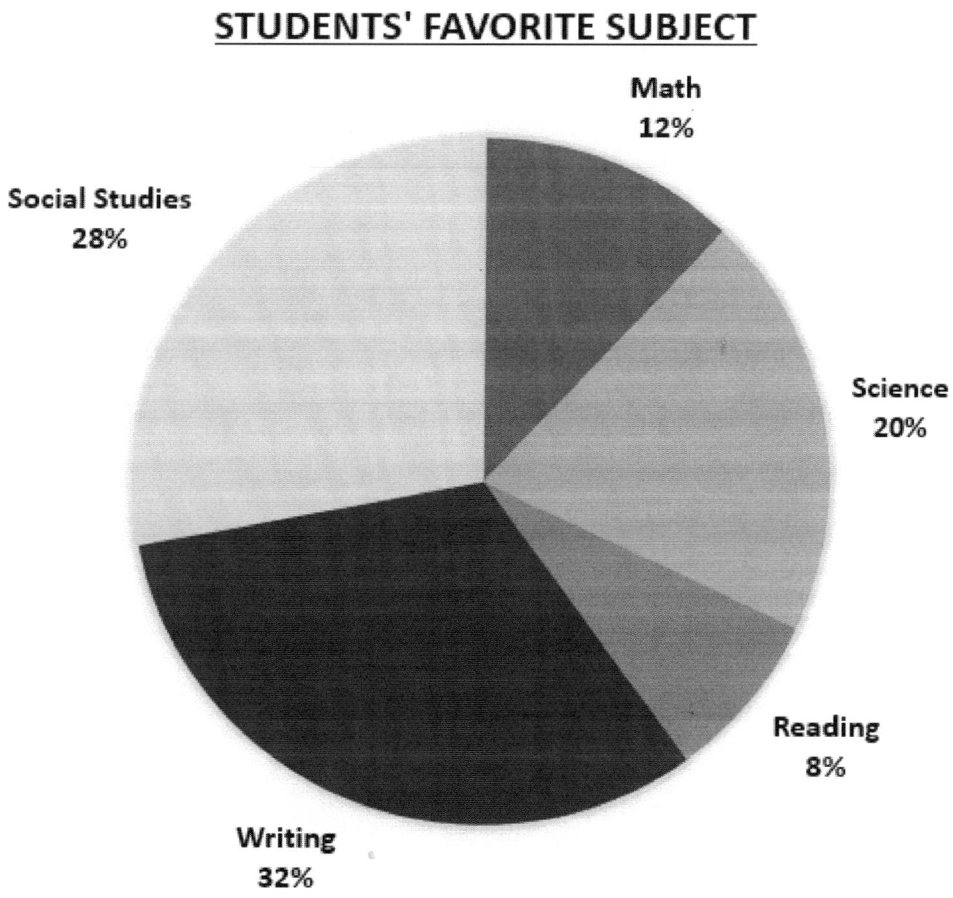

Lesson 11

Reading Pie Charts

1. pancakes
2. ham
3. bacon
4. ham
5. bacon
6. pancakes
7. eggs

Chapter 8—Money & Time

Lesson 1

Counting Money 1

1. 76¢
2. 72¢
3. $1.55
4. $1.86
5. 93¢
6. $1.81
7. $1.36
8. $1.09
9. $1.45

Counting Money 2

1. $1.41
2. $3.12
3. $7.61
4. $30.18
5. $25.87
6. $35.33

Lesson 2

Making Change 1

1. 25¢
2. 23¢
3. 36¢
4. 52¢
5. $3.93
6. $3.64
7. $4.36

Making Change 2

1. $3.95
2. $2.39
3. $1.68
4. $4.39
5. $3.91
6. $6.79
7. $9.19
8. $13.20

LESSON 3

WRITING MONEY

1. thirty-eight dollars and fifty-nine cents
2. one-hundred dollars and thirty-two cents
3. two-hundred seventy-eight dollars and twelve cents
4. three-hundred fifteen dollars and eight cents
5. nine-hundred fifteen dollars and eighty-three cents
6. eighteen dollars and thirty-three cents
7. two-hundred twenty-nine dollars and twenty-nine cents
8. seven-hundred fifty-six dollars and ten cents
9. six-hundred eighteen dollars and twenty-four cents
10. nine-hundred ninety-nine dollars and seventy-two cents

LESSON 4
TIME MATCHING

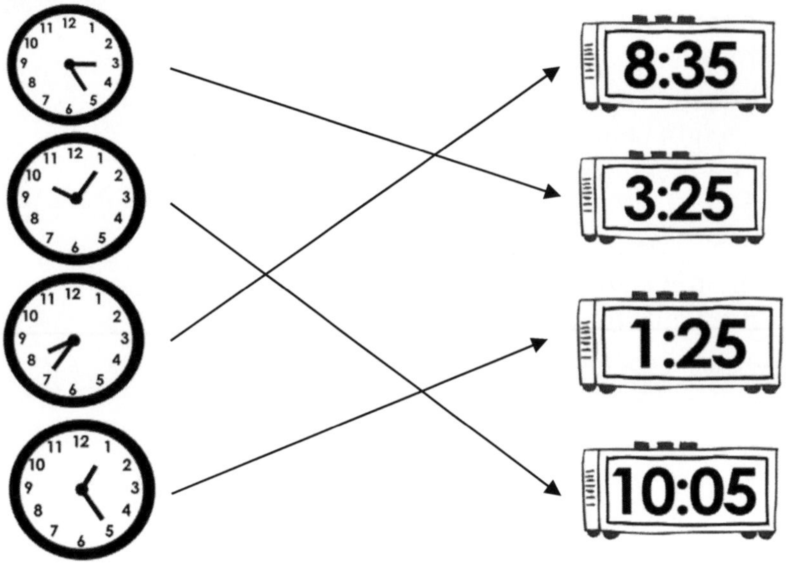

LESSON 5
AM & PM

1. AM
2. PM
3. AM
4. PM
5. PM
6. AM
7. PM
8. PM
9. AM
10. PM

Lesson 6

Adding and Subtracting Time

1. 6 hours 45 minutes

2. 9 hours 26 minutes

3. 5 hours 12 minutes

4. 15 hours 52 minutes

5. 3 hours 45 minutes

6. 1 hour 54 minutes

7. 58 minutes

8. 3 hours 48 minutes

LESSON 7

TIME PASSAGE 1

What time will it be in 3 hours and 15 minutes?

What time will it be in 2 hours and 30 minutes?

What time will it be in 1 hour and 45 minutes?

What time will it be in 2 hours and 15 minutes?

What time will it be in 4 hours and 45 minutes?

What time will it be in 3 hours and 30 minutes?

What time will it be in 5 hours and 45 minutes?

What time will it be in 1 hour and 15 minutes?

TIME PASSAGE 2

 What time will it be in 2 hours and 20 minutes?	 What time will it be in 1 hour and 35 minutes?
 What time will it be in 3 hours and 5 minutes?	 What time will it be in 6 hours and 10 minutes?
 What time will it be in 3 hours and 25 minutes?	 What time will it be in 3 hours and 15 minutes?
 What time will it be in 5 hours and 35 minutes?	 What time will it be in 3 hours and 15 minutes?

Chapter 9—Geometry & Measurements

Lesson 1

Shape Counting 1

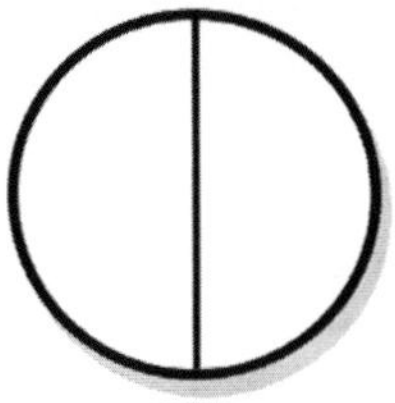

2

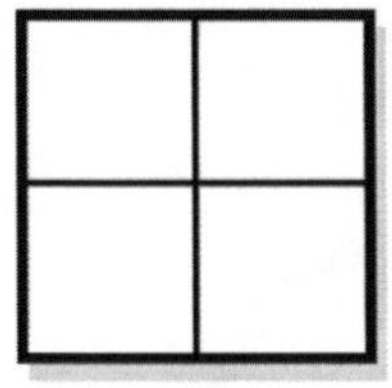

4

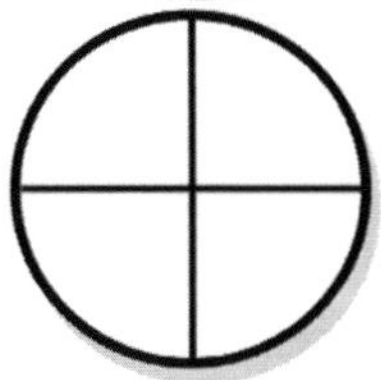

4

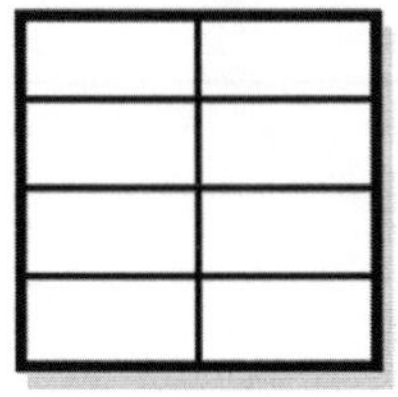

8

3

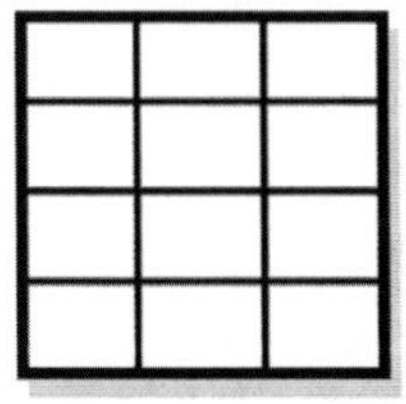

12

8

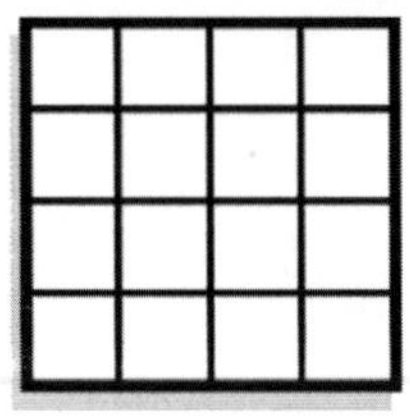

16

SHAPE COUNTING 2

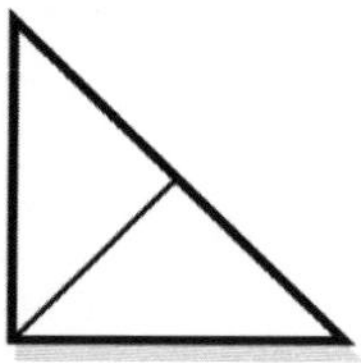

2

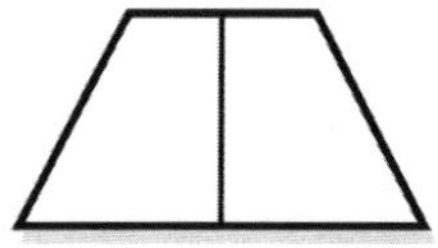

2

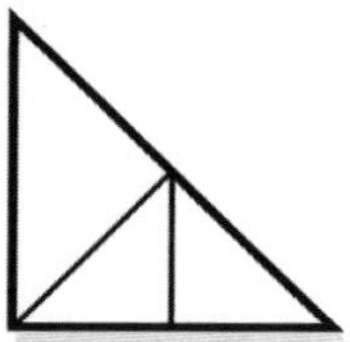

4

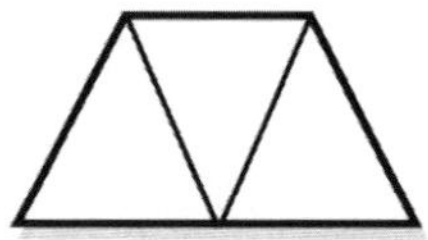

3

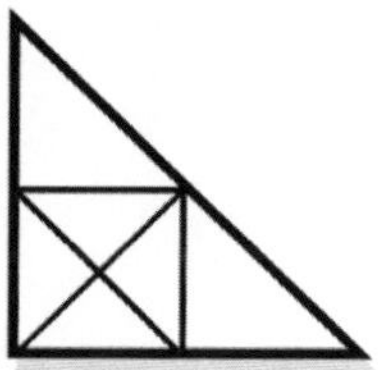

6

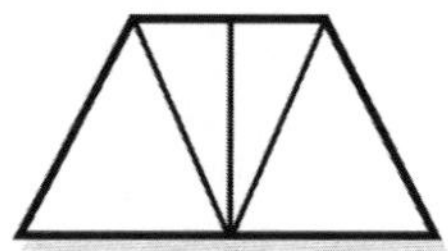

4

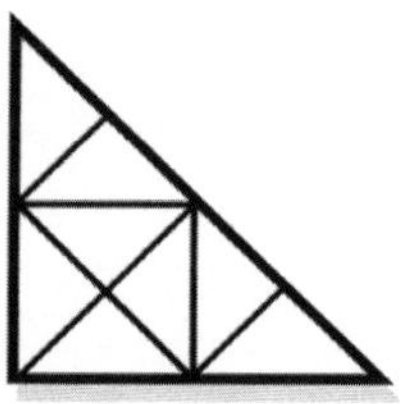

8

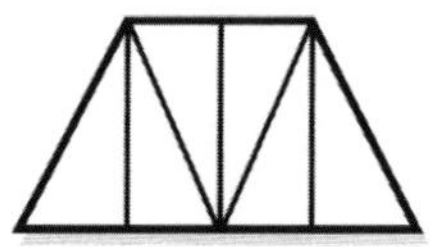

6

LESSON 2

COMPARING SHAPES BY SIDES

1. 1

2. 5

3. 10

4. 3

5. 11

Lesson 3

Lines of Symmetry

1.

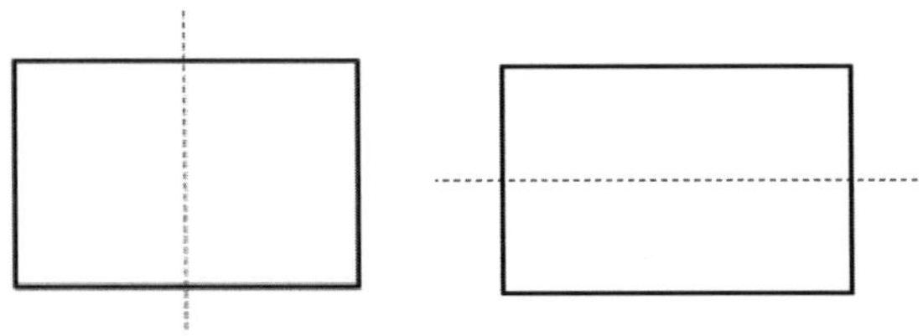

2.

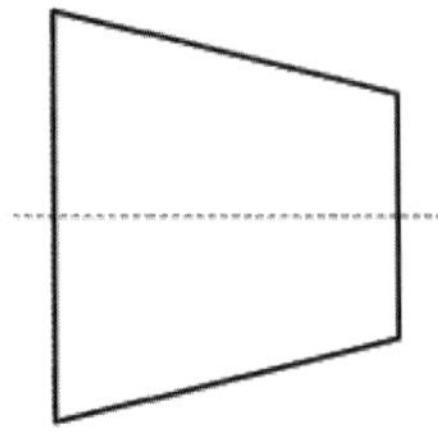

3.

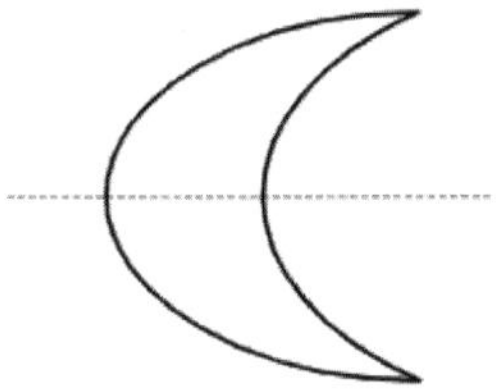

4.

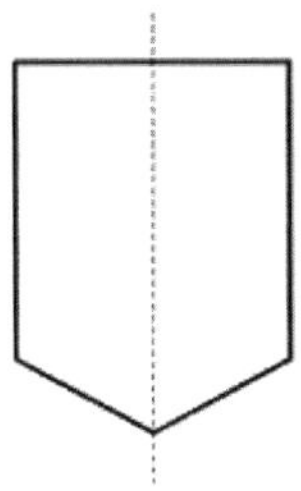

5.

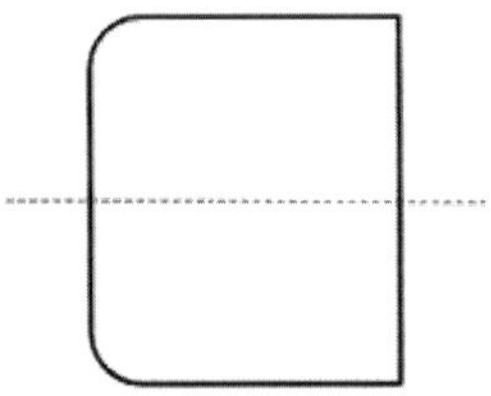

6.

Lesson 4

Area 1

1. 3
2. 4
3. 6
4. 7
5. 4
6. 7
7. 7

AREA 2

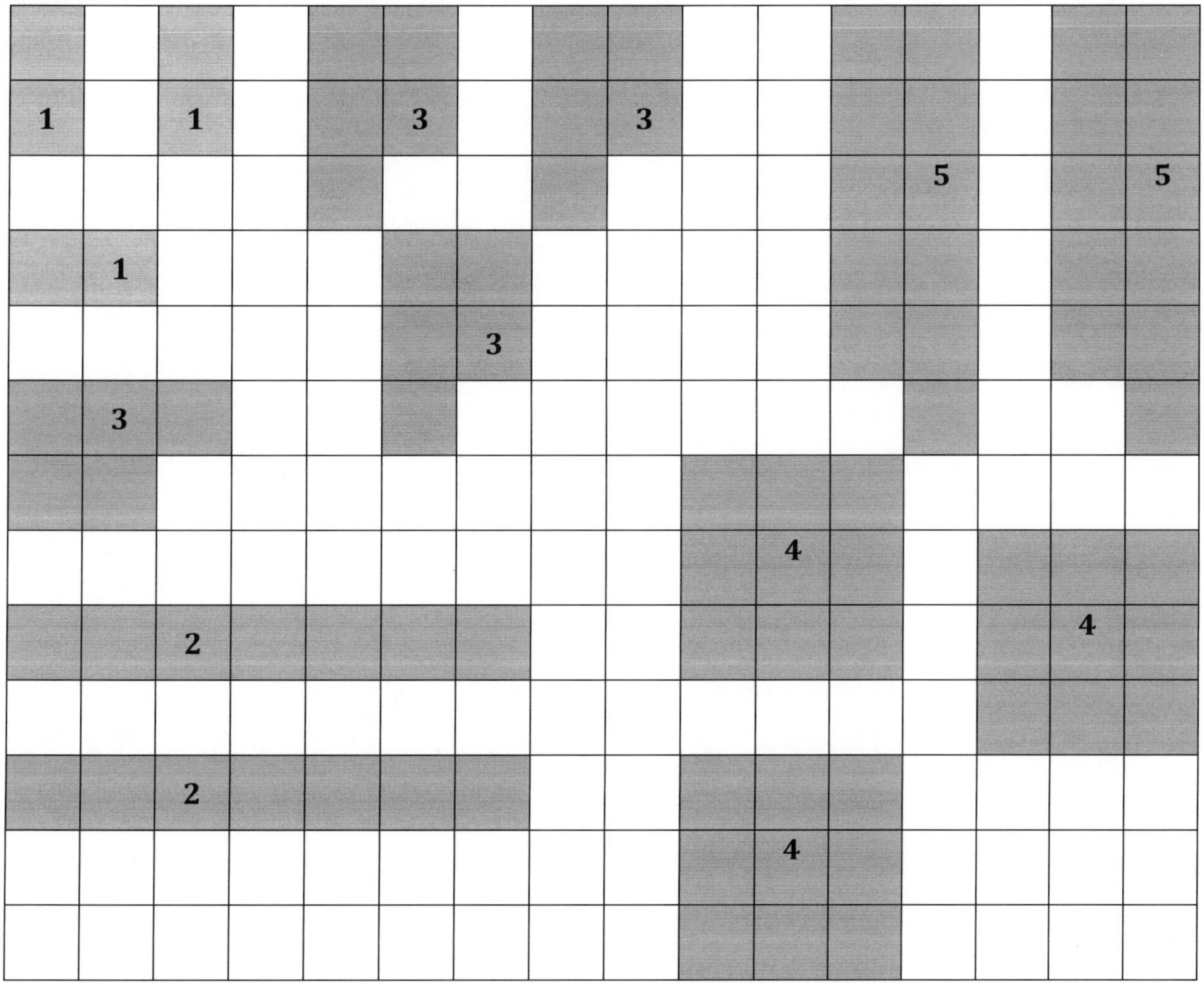

Lesson 5

Perimeter 1

1. 4 + 6 + 4 + 6 = 20 in

2. 7 + 7 + 7 = 21 ft

3. 8 + 20 + 20 + 26 = 74 in

4. 12 + 8 + 12 + 8 = 40 ft

5. 6 + 6 + 9 + 6 + 9 = 36 in

Perimeter 2

1. 8

2. 10

3. 9

4. 12

5. 10

6. 12

7. 14

Perimeter 3

Perimeter is the distance around a two-dimensional shape.

Use the grid to draw the shapes for each question.

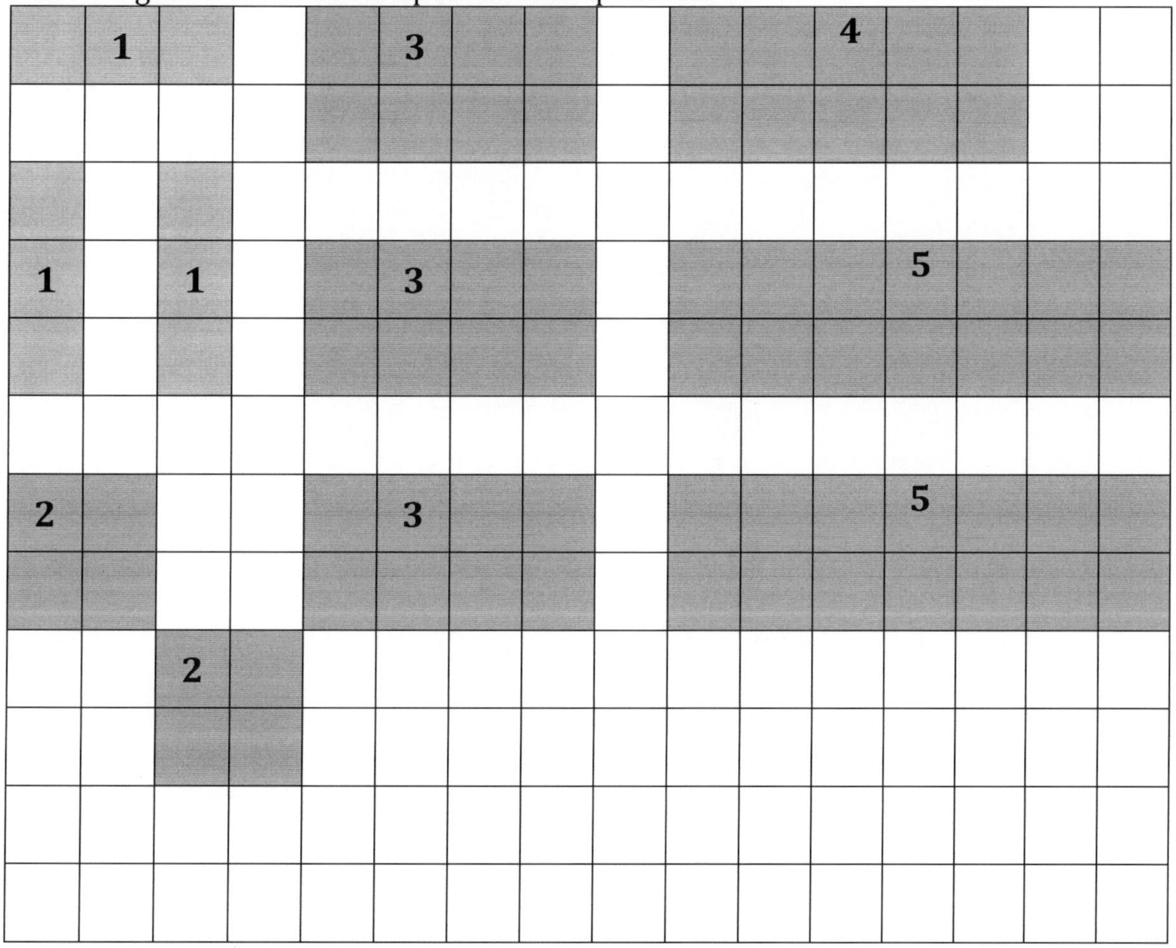

Lesson 6

Area Using a Formula

1. 84

2. 112

3. 45

4. 132

Lesson 7

Lines and Line Segments

1. line segment

2. point

3. line

4. line segment

5. XY or DF

6. line segment

7. Any point on the illustration

8. line

9. E

Lesson 8

Angles

1. Obtuse

2. Acute

3. Right

4. Obtuse

Lesson 9

Weight Measurements

1. Ounces

2. Pounds

3. Ounces

4. Pounds

5. Pounds

6. Ounces

Lesson 10

Distance Measurements

1. Yards

2. Feet

3. Miles

4. Feet

5. Feet

6. Miles

7. Feet

8. Yards

9. Miles

10. Foot

Lesson 11

Liquid Measurements

1. Cup

2. Gallon

3. Pint

4. Quart

5. Pint

6. Gallon

Answer Key and Explanations for Test #1

1. D: The annual expenses for Years 2009, 2007, 2008, 2011, and 2010 are $1,046, $1,224, $1,319, $1,342, and $1,529, respectively. These amounts are listed in order from lowest to highest. Since all of the numbers have a 1 in the thousands place, the numerals in the hundreds place must be compared. For the amounts of $1,319 and $1,342, the numerals in the tens place must be compared. No other choice shows the years listed in increasing order of expense.

2. B: The number, 860,002 has an 8 in the hundred-thousands place, a 6 in the ten-thousands place, a 0 in the thousands place, a 0 in the hundreds place, a 0 in the tens place, and a 2 in the ones place. The 860 written in front of the comma represents, "Eight hundred sixty thousand." The 2 in the ones place represents, "Two." Therefore, the number is read, "Eight hundred sixty thousand, two."

3. B: If $\frac{1}{3}$ of the balls Wyatt received were basketballs that means the remaining balls he received must have been soccer balls. Since the fraction used is $\frac{1}{3}$, look at it as if he received 3 balls. One ball was a basketball and the remaining balls had to be soccer balls. This is now a simple subtraction problem. 3 – 1 = 2 soccer balls.

4. D: The numbers: 608, 458, 452, 381, 321, and 294 are written in order from greatest to least. An examination of the numerals in the hundreds place reveals that 608 is the greatest and 294 is the least. The numbers, 458 and 452, are greater than the numbers, 381 and 321, based on the value of the digits in the hundreds place. An examination of the numerals in the ones place, since both the digits in the hundreds and the tens places are the same, allows you to compare 458 and 452, which shows 458 to be the larger number. An examination of the numerals in the tens place allows you to compare 381 and 321, since the digits in the hundreds place are the same, which shows 381 to be the larger number. None of the other choices show the numbers in descending order.

5. C: Choice C shows 2 triangles and 4 hexagons, which is a total of 6 shapes. The fraction 2 out of 6, or $\frac{2}{6}$, also represents 1 out of 3, or $\frac{1}{3}$. None of the other choices represent this fraction: Choice A shows $\frac{3}{6}$, which equals $\frac{1}{2}$. Choice B shows $\frac{1}{4}$. Choice D shows $\frac{1}{6}$.

6. 60: This is a simple multiplication problem which involves carrying the excess (greater than a single digit) to the next column. Start with the 5 and multiply each digit above: 5 x 2 = 10. Write down the 0 and place the 1 on top of the 1. Multiply 5 x 1 to get 5. Add in the 1 to get 6. Write down the number 6 and the product is 60.

7. D: The total number of feet he ascended can be determined by adding 482 feet and 362 feet. The sum of 482 and 362 is 844. Thus, he ascended 844 feet in all.

8. A: Grace has $12 + 12 = 24$ photos. These 24 photos need to be divided into groups of 4. Divide to find the number of pages required: $24 \div 4 = 6$. This means that 6 pages are required.

9. B: Choice B shows 4 shaded sections out of 6 total sections. The fraction, $\frac{4}{6}$, is the same as the fraction, $\frac{2}{3}$. Two shaded sections represent one-third of the total. Thus, four shaded sections represent two-thirds of the total. Each of the pictures has 6 total sections, so the other choices can be written as fractions with a 6 in the denominator. Choice A shows $\frac{3}{6}$, which equals $\frac{1}{2}$. Choice C shows . Choice D shows $\frac{2}{6}$, which equals $\frac{1}{3}$. So, only Choice B shows the correct picture.

10. D: A possible first step would be to divide the number of tiles glued each day by the number of hours it took to glue the tiles. The two quotients would then represent approximately how many tiles glued per hour, and could then be compared.

11. 54: Begin with the tokens given to each guest, which was 12. But the problem states that every game takes two tokens, so each guest can play only 6 games, not 12. Multiply this by the number of guests, 9, to equal 54 games.

12. C: Each number is 8 more than the previous number, which means that the next number can be found by adding 8 to the previous number. Thus, the fifth number is 353, the sixth number is 361, the seventh number is 369, and the eighth number is 377.

13. C: Each figure has 3 more squares than the previous figure, so adding 3 to the number of squares in the previous figure yields the number of squares in the next figure. Thus, he will use 14 squares for Figure 5, 17 squares for Figure 6, 20 squares for Figure 7, 23 squares for Figure 8, and 26 squares for Figure 9.

14. C: In order to find the amount donated the following year, you multiply the amount donated the previous year by 3. Thus, the amount donated the second year was \$6 (\$2 $\times$ 3). The amount donated the third year was \$18 (\$6 $\times$ 3). The amount donated the fourth year was \$54 (\$18 $\times$ 3). The amount donated the fifth year was \$162 (\$54 $\times$ 3).

15. 4: Since $12 \div 3 = 4$, it also true that $4 \times 3 = 12$. These three numbers are fact families; therefore, four times three equals twelve, three times four equals twelve, twelve divided by three equals four, and twelve divided by four equals three.

16. D: Each spider has 8 legs. In order to find the number of legs present with 3 spiders, you multiply 3 by 8, which is 24. Thus, 3 spiders have 24 legs in all. Choice D is the only table that shows each number of spiders, multiplied by 8, to yield the correct product representing the total number of legs.

17. C: Each candy jar has 14 pieces of candy. This can be determined by dividing the number of pieces of candy by the number of candy jars: $28 \div 2 = 14, 56 \div 4 = 14, 70 \div 5 = 14, 126 \div 9 = 14$. Since the data in the table shows that there are 14 pieces of candy in each jar, multiplying $13 \times 14 = 182$ finds the total number of pieces of candy that are in 13 candy jars.

18. C: Penny drank 96 glasses of water over the course of 12 days. Since $96 \div 12 = 8$, it can be determined that Penny drank about 8 glasses per day on average. Since these three numbers are in the same fact family, the number sentence can be rewritten several ways:

$$96 \div 8 = 12$$

$$8 \times 12 = 96$$

$$12 \times 8 = 96$$

Therefore, $12 \times ? = 96$ is the only other number sentence that would also determine how many glasses of water Penny drank each day.

19. B: $\frac{3}{5}$ is less than $\frac{4}{5}$. They are not equal. When comparing fractions with the same denominator, compare only the values in the numerator. Since they share a common denominator of 5, compare only the 3 and 4. Since 3 is less than 4, the same can be said for the fraction $\frac{3}{5}$ when compared to $\frac{4}{5}$.

20. A: Each box of chocolates is made up of 24 chocolates. 3 boxes contain $24 + 24 + 24$, which simplifies to 72. Repeated addition is also known as multiplication, so $24 \times 3 = 72$ There are 72 pieces of chocolate in 3 boxes.

21. D: $12\frac{1}{4}$ is represented by the first tick mark to the right of the 12. $12\frac{2}{4}$ is the second tick mark and $12\frac{3}{4}$ is the third tick mark, or the tick mark before the 13. Only $12\frac{3}{4}$ appears to the right of point M on the number line, making it greater.

22. B: Fractions are considered equivalent if they represent the same distance from 0 on a number line. $\frac{2}{6}$ can be simplified to $\frac{1}{3}$ by dividing the top and bottom of the fraction by 3. The location of $\frac{1}{3}$ will be at the same location as $\frac{2}{6}$.

23. B: It can be determined that $\frac{2}{3}$ is equivalent to $\frac{10}{15}$ by multiplying both the numerator and denominator of $\frac{2}{3}$ by the same factor. Since $2 \times 5 = 10$, the denominator, 3, needs to also be multiplied by the factor of 5. Since 3×5 does indeed equal 15, it can be concluded that the two fractions are equivalent. If multiplying the denominator by the same factor as the numerator of the first fraction does not provide the same product as in the denominator of the second fraction, the two fractions cannot be equivalent.

24. C: What number times 9 equals 72? Or how many groups of 9 are needed to reach 72? The missing number is 8. So, $8 \times 9 = 72$. 8 groups of 9 are needed to reach 72.

25. $\frac{1}{6}$: Unit fractions have 1 in the numerator. For example, $\frac{1}{2}, \frac{1}{3}, \frac{1}{4}, \frac{1}{5}$, and $\frac{1}{6}$ are unit fractions. When one whole is divided into 6 equal shares, each share represents 1 out of 6, or the unit fraction $\frac{1}{6}$.

26. B: Each increment represents one-half. This can be determined by counting that there are 3 marks, or 4 spaces, that lie between the difference of two wholes, as in between 10 and 12. Thus, one increment past 10, where Point P is located, represents $10\frac{1}{2}$.

27. D: A trapezoid has 4 sides. Two of the sides are parallel to each other. This means that if the lines continued forever, they would never touch or intersect. The other two sides are not parallel.

28. B: The perimeter is the distance around the figure. To calculate this, add up all of the side lengths. Since a rectangle has two pairs of congruent sides, the opposite sides have the same length as the measurements already given. Therefore, $8 + 8 + 13 + 13 = 42$, so the perimeter is 42 units.

29. A: To find the product of 30 and 6, multiply 6 and 0 together. The product of this is 0, and that will be the digit in the ones places of the final product. Then multiply 3 and 6 together to get a product of 18. The 1 will be the digit in the hundreds places, and the 8 will be the digit in the tens place. Therefore, the final product of 30 and 6 is 180.

30. C: The width of the rectangle is given as 6 in., and the length can be found by multiplying that times 3. Thus, $6 \times 3 = 18$. To find the area of a rectangle, multiply the length times the width, so $6 \times 18 = 108$. Area is always measured in square units, so the units will be in^2.

31. B: There are 4 shaded sections and 6 sections total. 4 out of 6 simplifies to 2 out of 3. $\frac{4}{6}$ is equivalent to $\frac{2}{3}$ because $\frac{4}{6}$ becomes $\frac{2}{3}$ when the numerator and denominator are divided by 2.

32. B: The thermometer shows the temperature to be very close to 102 degrees Fahrenheit. It also shows the temperature in Celsius which is about 40 degrees.

33. C: The short hand, or hour hand, is between 12 o'clock and 1 o'clock, revealing that Karen went to the library after 12 o'clock. The long hand, or minute hand, is pointed at the 3. Since the 3 on the clock represents 15 minutes after the hour (since each number shown on the clock represents 5 minutes and $3 \times 5 = 15$), the clock shows that Karen went to the library at 12:15.

34. B: There are 16 small squares in total. This means that for $\frac{5}{8}$ of them to be shaded there would need to be 10 of them shaded.

35. C: To find out how long it takes Ashley to get ready just add up all of the minutes that she spends doing various activities. $6 + 7 + 12 + 2 = 27$

36. D: Texas has the most zoos because it has 15 zoos, while the other states each have 7 zoos, 4 zoos, and 11 zoos. Also, it can be seen from the graph that the bar representing Texas is much higher than the bars for the other states.

37. D: Choices A, B, and C, have a missing value of 8. Choice D has a missing value of 10, so it does not belong with the rest.

$$7 \times \mathbf{8} = 56$$

$$\mathbf{8} \times 1 = 8$$

$$3 \times \mathbf{8} = 24$$

$$4 \times \mathbf{10} = 40$$

38. B: The figure shown is an isosceles trapezoid, and it has 1 line of symmetry, which is a vertical line that passes through the midpoint of each base. Therefore, it goes directly through the middle from top to bottom. Symmetry is when an image can be folded on itself and is an identical mirror image.

39. C: Baseball received 6 votes and basketball received only 2 votes. The difference is 6 – 2 = 4 fewer votes.

40. A: Since each tree represents 2 lawns, the pictograph shows that the number of lawns finished by Company A is equal to 6×2, or 12 lawns, the number of lawns finished by Company B is equal to 9×2, or 18 lawns, the number of lawns finished by Company C is equal to 3×2, or 6 lawns, and the number of lawns finished by Company D is equal to 8×2, or 16 lawns. This is the only pictograph that represents the correct number of lawns.

Answer Key and Explanations for Test #2

1. D: There are 8 shelves with 16 books on each shelf. This represents a multiplication scenario. Consider using the standard algorithm.

$$\begin{array}{r} {}^{4} \\ 16 \\ \times\ 8 \\ \hline 128 \end{array}$$

8 times 6 is 48. Write 4 above the 1 and 8 on the answer line. Now multiply 8 times 1, and add 4. This is 12. Write 12 on the answer line. The product is 128, so there is a total of 128 books.

2. D: Choice D shows 1 crayon and 3 pencils, indicating that 1 out of 4 of Camille's writing tools were crayons. The other choices are out of either a total of 7 writing tools or 5 writing tools, which cannot be used in a ratio that represents 1 out of 4.

3. D: In order to find out the total number of hot dogs she sold in the two months, the amount sold in each month should be added. The sum of 128 and 117 is 245. Thus, she sold 245 hot dogs during the two months.

4. B: There are 4 equal parts between 0 and 1 on the number line. The dot represents 1 part out of 4 parts, or the fraction $\frac{1}{4}$. The dot is one-quarter of the distance between 0 to 1.

5. C: The difference between the two depths can be determined using subtraction based on place value.

$$\begin{array}{r} 16 \\ 8\ \ 6/16 \\ \not{9}\not{7}\not{7} \\ -779 \\ \hline 198 \end{array}$$

6. D: The dark region shows 4 out of 8 pieces. $\frac{4}{8}$ can be simplified to $\frac{1}{2}$. 4 is the greatest common multiple of 4 and 8, so divide the numerator and denominator of $\frac{4}{8}$ by 4. $\frac{4}{8}$ becomes $\frac{1}{2}$, which is in simplest form.

7. C: The factors 6 times 8 has a product of 48.

All of the other factors have a product of 56.

$$14 \times 4 = 56$$

$$2 \times 28 = 56$$

$$8 \times 7 = 56$$

8. B: Each model shows a whole, split into 7 sections. This makes the denominator equal to 7 for the fraction representing the shaded section for each. Since the fractions all have the same number on the bottom, the number of shaded sections can be compared. For a fraction to be more than $\frac{4}{7}$, more than 4 parts must be shaded. The model shown for Choice B shows the fraction $\frac{6}{7}$, because 6 out of 7 sections are shaded, showing a fraction that is more than 4 out of 7. The other choices all show either 4 parts or less than 4 parts shaded.

9. B: The sequence of the number of miles walked in order from greatest to least is: 963 (Year 4), 691 (Year 1), 567 (Year 2), 221 (Year 5), 144 (Year 3). The number of miles walked can also be compared by examining only the digits in the hundreds place since they are all different. 9 is greater than 6 which is greater than 5 and so on. The only choice that shows the years for the number of miles walked in descending order is B.

10. C: Fact families relate multiplication and division. A fact family consist of the same 3 numbers, and creates 2 multiplication equations and 2 division equations. For example, $48 \div 8 = 6$,

$48 \div 6 = 8$, $6 \times 8 = 48$, and $8 \times 6 = 48$ create a fact family. Multiplication can be used to solve division problems using fact families. $6 \times 8 = 48$, which means the missing number in $48 \div 8 = \_\_\_$ is 6.

11. A: To find the answer reduce the fractions to their lowest terms. For answer choice A, $\frac{4}{6}$, both the numerator and denominator can be divided by 2 to get $\frac{2}{3}$.

12. B: Looking at all the answer choices, the numerators are all the same. When comparing fractions with the same numerators, the ones with a larger denominator are smaller in value than the ones with a smaller denominator. This is because the whole is divided into more pieces than the one with the smaller denominator; thus, its value is smaller. To find the fraction that is bigger than $\frac{5}{8}$, the denominator needs to be smaller than 8. Therefore, the only option is choice B, $\frac{5}{6}$.

13. B: The farmer plants 17 rows of corn each season. This can be found using all of the information given in the table. The farmer had planted 34 rows of corn by the end of Season 2 and 68 rows of corn by the end of Season 4, indicating an increase of 34 rows of corn between the two seasons. So, by dividing 34 by 2, the numbers of rows planted in one season is found. Also, the farmer had planted 102 rows of corn by the end of Season 6 and 119 rows of corn by the end of Season 7, indicating an increase of 17 rows of corn planted in one season. If 17 rows of corn are added to the number given at the end of Season 2, the result is 51 rows of corn planted by the end of Season 3. If another 17 rows of corn are added to this amount, the farmer would have planted 68 ears of corn by the end of Season 4, which he did. Thus, he did plant 17 rows of corn each year. He had planted 136 rows of corn by the end of Season 8, 153 rows of corn by the end of Season 9, and 170 rows of corn by the end of Season 10.

14. 35 cm: To find the area of a rectangle just multiply the length times the width.

15. A: Each block represents 1,000. There are two blocks so this represents 2,000. Each flat square represents 100. There are 4 flat squares so this represents 400. Each rod represents 10. There are 5 rods so this represents 50. Each small cube represents 1. There are 9 small cubes so this represents 9. When all of these values are combined, they form the expression $2{,}000 + 400 + 50 + 9$, which is in expanded form.

16. D: The number of books brought by 2 students is 8, while the number of books brought by 5 students and 6 students increased by 4. Thus, the number of books brought by each student was 4. This fact can be checked by starting with 1 student and 4 books brought, and continuing the pattern to make sure it corresponds with the numbers in the table. For example, 8 students brought 32, which does in fact agree with the each student bringing 4 books. So, the number of books each student brought, 4, is multiplied by the number of students to find the total number of books that were brought. Thus, 12 students brought 12×4 books, or 48 books.

17. 164: Calculate the total height of the friends by adding all three heights together: $60 + 58 + 46 = 164$. Therefore, the total height of the friends is 164 inches.

18. D: A line of symmetry is a line that can be drawn through a shape such that the remaining part of the shape on either side of the line looks the same, but is reflected. The shape shown is a hexagon, and it has 6 lines of symmetry.

19. B: If the number in the ones place is even, then the entire number is even. 8 is in the ones place, and 8 is even. Therefore, 138 is even.

According to the rules of divisibility, any number with an even digit in the ones place is an even number. 138 has an 8 in the ones place, and 8 is even because it can be split into 2 equal groups, so 138 is even.

20. C: Every fact family has three numbers. Fact families can be built into two multiplication scenarios and two division scenarios. The same three numbers are used in all three scenarios. $48 \div 8 = 6$ is the missing division equation.

21. 185: She starts with 152 stickers and then gives 34 away. So, 152-34=118. Then she buys 67 more, which gives her 118+67=185.

22. B: The number of customers who entered the store can be rounded to 90. That number can be multiplied by 3, since each customer receives 6 coupons. The product of 90×3 is 270.

23. D: Figures A, B, and C can all be folded in a manner that the squares lay directly on top of each other. This cannot be done with Figure D; therefore, Figure D does not have a line of symmetry.

24. C: Now count the boxes that are shaded in and you get 6, so $\frac{6}{11}$ are shaded.

25. B: The area of a rectangle is found by multiplying length times width. In this problem you are given the area and the width and asked to find length *x*. To find this divide 36 by 4 to get 9.

26. C: Each number is 7 more than the previous number, so adding 7 to the previous number finds the next number. Thus, the fifth number is 256, the sixth number is 263, and the seventh number is 270.

27. C: One way to compare two fractions is by making two strip diagrams. The denominator represents how many equal spaces the strip will be divided into. The numerator represents how many spaces on the strip will be shaded in. It is important to make the strip diagrams the same size to accurately compare the fractions. When looking at the strip diagrams, it is evident that $\frac{1}{3}$ is greater than $\frac{1}{12}$.

$\frac{1}{12}$

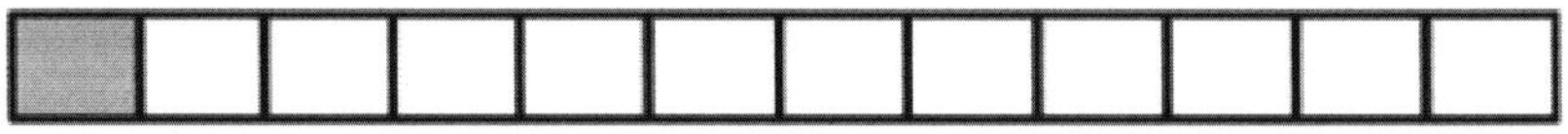

$\frac{1}{3}$

28. 180: To find the total number of minutes he reads multiply 6 times 30 to get 180.

29. B: The total weight of the watermelons was 28, and if each one weighed the same then you can just divide by 7 to get 4 pounds each.

30. D: The rectangle includes 66 whole square units. The rectangle is 6 units by 11 units. When finding the area of a rectangle, the formula is length × width, so $6 \times 11 = 66$.

31. D: $\frac{6}{14}$ is the only value that comes between $\frac{3}{14}$ and $\frac{7}{14}$ on the number line. $\frac{1}{14}$ is less than $\frac{3}{14}$, so it is before $\frac{3}{14}$ on the number line. $\frac{3}{14}$ is equal to $\frac{3}{14}$, so it is at the exact place on the number line. $\frac{9}{14}$ is greater than $\frac{3}{14}$, so it is after $\frac{3}{14}$ on the number line.

32. C: To find how much total time John spent walking, add the time together. 9 minutes plus 12 minutes plus 23 minutes equals 44 minutes, $9 + 12 + 23 = 44$. Therefore, John walked for a total of 44 minutes from the time he left his house until he returned home.

33. A: The short hand, or hour hand, is between 10 o'clock and 11 o'clock, revealing that Amanda arrived after 10 o'clock, but before 11 o'clock. It is much closer to the 10, so this indicates the time is much closer to 10 o'clock than 11 o'clock. The long hand, or minute hand, is pointing to the 2, indicating 10 minutes after the hour. This is because for minutes, each number represents 5 minutes; so $2 \times 5 = 10$. So, she arrived at the party at 10:10.

34. C: $\frac{9}{12}$ is greater than $\frac{7}{12}$. They are not equal. When comparing fractions with the same denominator, compare only the values in the numerator. Since they share a common denominator of 12, compare only the 9 and 7. Since 9 is greater than 7, the same can be said for the fraction $\frac{9}{12}$ when compared to $\frac{7}{12}$.

35. D: The thermometer shows 4 marks between each whole number, or 5 intervals. This means each interval on the thermometer represents 2 degrees since there are 5 intervals between each difference of 10 degrees. The thermometer reveals a reading at 4 degrees above 70 degrees (2 marks above 70), or 6 degrees below 80 degrees (3 marks below 80). Thus, the temperature outside is 74 degrees Fahrenheit.

36. A: The number 13 can be expanded to $10 + 3$. Then, using distributive property, 4 can be multiplied by 10 and also multiplied by 3. The two products will be added together.

$$4 \times (10 + 3)$$
$$(4 \times 10) + (4 \times 3)$$
$$40 + 12$$
$$52$$

Since the result is 52, the product to 4 and 13 is also equal to 52.

37. C: Florida had 20 teachers that attended the event, which is less than the number of teachers who attended the event from each of the other three states. The number of teachers that attended the event from each of the other states were 40 (Arizona), 80 (New York), and 50 (California). Also, just looking at the bar graph shows that Florida had the least number of teachers attend compared to the other states because the bar is much lower in the graph.

38. A: The pictograph for Choice A reveals that each picture of a cake represents 5 actual cakes. Therefore, the numbers given in the table, divided by 5, should equal the number of cakes represented in the pictograph. The pictograph accurately shows 5 cakes for 25 actual cakes, 3 cakes for 15 actual cakes, 7 cakes for 35 actual cakes, and 4 cakes for 20 actual cakes. This is the only pictograph that represents the correct number of cakes.

39. 8: The hamster received 10 votes and the fish received 2 votes. The difference is 10 – 2 = 8.

40. C: Parallel lines are lines that will never intersect if they continue forever. A trapezoid only has one set of parallel lines. A triangle does not have any parallel lines. A rectangle and a square both have two sets of parallel lines.

Online Resources

Due to our efforts to try to keep this book to a manageable length, we've created a link that will give you access to all of your online resources:

mometrix.com/resources719/flg3mathwb

It's Your Moment, Let's Celebrate It!

Share your story @mometrixtestpreparation